Crossway Bible

Series editors: Ian Coffey (NT), Stephen Gaukroger (OT)
Old Testament editor: Stephen Dray
New Testament editor: Steve Motyer

Titles in this series

Genesis, Richard and Tricia Johnson
Exodus, Stephen Dray
Leviticus, Derek Tidball
Joshua, Charles Price
Ruth and Esther, Debra Reid
Ezra and Nehemiah, Dave Cave
Psalms 1 – 72, Alan Palmer
Psalms 73 – 150, Alan Palmer and Debra Reid
Isaiah, Philip Hacking
Six Minor Prophets, Michael Wilcock
Haggai, Zechariah and Malachi, John James
Matthew's Gospel, Stephen Dray
Mark's Gospel, David Hewitt
Luke's Gospel, Simon Jones
John's Gospel, Ian Barclay
Acts, Stephen Gaukroger
Romans, David Coffey
1 Corinthians, Robin Dowling and Stephen Dray
2 Corinthians, Jonathan Lamb
Ephesians, Steve Motyer
Philippians, Ian Coffey
Colossians and Philemon, Stephen Gaukroger and
Derek Wood
1 & 2 Thessalonians, Alec Motyer and Steve Motyer
Timothy and Titus, Michael Griffiths
James, David Field
1 Peter, Andrew Whitman
John's Letters, Dianne Tidball

The Bible with Pleasure, Steve Motyer
Discovering the New Testament, Simon Jones
Housegroups: The Leaders' Survival Guide, Ian Coffey and
Stephen Gaukroger (eds.)
Rebuild, Fran Beckett (ed.)

John's Letters:
Crossway Bible Guide

Dianne Tidball

Crossway Books Leicester

CROSSWAY BOOKS
38 De Montfort Street, Leicester LE1 7GP, England
Email: ivp@uccf.org.uk
Website: www.ivpbooks.com

First published 2002

British Library Cataloguing in Publication Data
A catalogue record for this book is available from the British Library.

ISBN 1-85684-211-8

Set in Palatino

Typeset in Great Britain by Avocet Typeset, Brill, Aylesbury, Bucks
Printed in Great Britain by Cox & Wyman Ltd, Reading

To
Beryl Gray
and in memory of
Vic Gray
Proverbs 17:6b

CONTENTS

Three routes through the letters of John

If you are planning a series of Bible studies, here are three examples of selections.

Welcome!

These days, meeting together to study the Bible in groups appears to be a booming leisure-time activity in many parts of the world. In the United Kingdom alone, it is estimated that over one million people each week meet in home Bible-study groups.

This series has been designed to help such groups and, in particular, those who lead them. These Bible Guides are also very suitable for individual study, and may help hard-pressed preachers, teachers and students too (see 'How to use this Bible Guide', on the following page).

We have therefore enlisted authors who are in the business of teaching the Bible to others and are doing it well. They have kept in their sights two clear aims:

1. To explain and apply the message of the Bible in non-technical language.
2. To encourage discussion, prayer and action on what the Bible teaches.

All of us engaged in the project believe that the Bible is the Word of God – given to us in order that people might discover him and his purposes for our lives. We believe that the sixty-six books which go to make up the Bible, although written by different people, in different places, at different times, through different circumstances, have a single unifying theme: that theme is Salvation. This means free forgiveness and the removal of all our guilt, it means the gift of eternal life, and it means the wholeness of purpose and joy which God has designed us to experience here and now, all of this being made possible through the Lord Jesus Christ.

How to use this Bible Guide

These guides have been prepared both for personal study and for the leaders and members of small groups. More information about group study follows on the next few pages.

You can use this book very profitably as a personal study guide. The short studies are ideal for daily reading: the first of the questions provided is usually aimed to help you with personal reflection (see 'How to tackle personal Bible study', below). If you prefer to settle down to a longer period of study, you can use groups of three to five studies, and thus get a better overview of a longer Bible passage. In either case, using the Bible Guide will help you to be disciplined about regular study, a habit that countless Christians have found greatly beneficial. (See also 'Three routes through the letters of John' on page 9 for methods of selecting studies if you do not intend to use them all.)

Yet a third use for these Bible Guides is as a quarry for ideas for the busy Bible teacher, providing outlines and application for those giving talks or sermons or teaching children. You will need more than this book can offer, of course, but the way the Bible text is broken down, comments are offered and questions are raised may well suggest directions to follow.

How to tackle personal Bible study

We have already suggested that you might use this book as a personal study guide. Now for some more detail.

One of the best methods of Bible study is to read the text through carefully several times, if possible using different versions or translations. Having reflected on the material, it is a good discipline to write down your own thoughts before doing anything else. At this stage it can be useful to consult another background book (see 'Resources' on page 14 and 'For further reading' on page 154). If you are using this book as your main study resource, then read through the relevant sections carefully, turning up the Bible references that are mentioned. The questions at the end of each chapter are specifically designed to help you to apply the passage to your own situation. You may find it helpful to write your answers to the questions in your notes.

It is a good habit to conclude with prayer, bringing before God the things you have learned.

If this kind of in-depth study is too demanding for you and you have only a short time at your disposal, read the Bible passage, read the comments in the Bible Guide, think round one of the questions and commit what you have learned to God in a brief prayer. This would take about fifteen minutes without rushing it.

How to tackle your group Bible study

1. Getting help

If you are new to leading groups, you will obviously want to get all the help you can from ministers and experienced friends. Books are also extremely helpful and we strongly recommend a book prepared by the editors of this series of Bible Guides: *Housegroups: The Leaders' Survival Guide*, edited by Ian Coffey and Stephen Gaukroger (Crossway Books, 1996). This book looks at the whole range of different types of group, asking what is the point of it all, what makes a good leader, how to tackle your meeting, how to help the members, how to study, pray, share and worship, and plenty of other pointers, tips and guidelines.

This book is a 'must' for all leaders of small groups. It is written by a team of people widely experienced in this area. It is available at your local Christian bookshop. If you have difficulty in obtaining a copy, write to Crossway

Books, Norton Street, Nottingham NG7 3HR, UK.

2. Planning a programme with your Bible Guide

This guide is a commentary on God's Word, written to help group members to get the most out of their studies. Although it is never ideal to chop up Scripture into small pieces, which its authors never intended, huge chunks are indigestible and we have tried to provide a diet of bite-sized mouthfuls.

The book is divided into major parts, each with a title indicated by a part-title page with a large number. If you want to get an overview of John's letters in a series of meetings you will need to select appropriate studies for each meeting. Read them yourself first and prepare a short summary of the studies you are tackling for your group. Ideally you could write it on a sheet of A5 paper and hand a copy to each member. Then choose one study from the part you are dealing with as a basis for your meeting. Do not attempt to pack more than one study into one meeting but choose the crucial one, the study which best crystallizes the message.

If you do not intend to cover the whole of John's letters, choose a series of studies to suit the number of meetings you have available. Each part of the commentary is divided into a few studies. It is a good idea to use consecutive studies, not to dodge about. You will then build up a detailed picture of one section of Scripture. Alternative examples of programmes of study are given in 'Three routes through the letters of John' on page 9.

3. Resources

You will find any or all of these books of great value in providing background to your Bible knowledge. Put some of them on your Christmas list and build up your library.

New Bible Dictionary or *New Concise Bible Dictionary* (IVP)
New Bible Atlas (IVP)
New Bible Commentary (21st Century edition) (IVP)
Handbook of Life in Bible Times, John Thompson (IVP)

The Bible User's Manual (IVP)
The Lion Handbook to the Bible (Lion Publishing)
The Message of the Bible (Lion Publishing)
NIV *Study Bible* (Hodder & Stoughton)
The Bible with Pleasure, Steve Motyer (Crossway Books)
Discovering the New Testament, Simon Jones (Crossway
   Books)

The relevant volume in the IVP Tyndale Commentary
series will give you reliable and detailed help with any
knotty points you may encounter.

4. Preparing to lead

Reading, discussing with friends, studying, praying,
reflecting on life ... preparation can be endless. But do not
be daunted by that. If you wait to become the perfect
leader you will never start at all. The really vital elements
in preparation are:

▶ prayer (not only in words but an attitude of dependence on God: 'Lord, I can't manage this on my own')

▶ familiarity with the study passage (careful reading of
   the text, the Bible Guide study and any other resource
   books that throw light on it) and

▶ a clear idea of where you hope to get in the meeting
   (notes on your introduction, perhaps, recap what was
   covered at the last meeting, and what direction you
   hope the questions will take you in – don't force the
   group to give your answers).

Here is a short checklist for the busy group leader:

Have I prayed about the meeting?
Have I decided exactly what I want to achieve
   through the meeting?
Have I prepared the material?
Am I clear about the questions that will encourage
   positive group discussion?

Am I gently encouraging silent members?

Am I, again gently, quietening the chatterers?

Am I willing to admit ignorance?

Am I willing to listen to what the group members say and to value their contributions?

Am I ready not to be dogmatic, not imposing my ideas on the group?

Have I planned how to involve the members in discovering for themselves?

Have I developed several 'prayer points' that will help focus the group?

Are we applying Scripture to our experience of real life or only using it as a peg to hang our opinions on?

Are we finding resources for action and change or just having a nice talk?

Are we all enjoying the experience together?

What do John's letters teach us?

The letters were written to a particular church situation where the believers had been misled by others. The letters are a corrective measure to ensure the church remains true to the basics of the gospel. In these letters we can expect to discover:

▶ The type of false understanding that was being taught about Jesus Christ and the gospel.

▶ How false teaching affects Christian living and causes problems in relationships.

▶ The basic truth about Jesus Christ, human and divine.

▶ A range of topics relevant to Christian life such as love, sin, assurance, worldliness, obedience, discernment and truth.

These letters may have been written 2,000 years ago in a

very different cultural and technological context to today. However, the themes and principles that the letters cover remain relevant because they are timeless issues of spiritual truth and human relationships.

Finding your way around this book

In our Bible Guides we have developed special symbols to make things easier to follow. Every study therefore has an opening section which is the passage in a nutshell.

The main section is the one that *makes sense of the passage*.

Questions

Every passage also has special questions for personal and group study after the main section. Some questions are addressed to us as individuals, some speak to us as members of our church or home group, while others concern us as members of God's people worldwide. The questions are deliberately designed

▶ to get people thinking about the passage

▶ to apply the text to 'real-life' situations

▶ to encourage reflection, discussion and action!

As a group leader you may well discover additional questions that will have special relevance to your group, so look out for these and note them in your preparation time.

Digging deeper

Some passages require an extra amount of explanation, and we have put these sections into different categories. The first kind gives additional background material that helps us to understand something factual. For example, if we dig deeper into the Gospels, it helps us to know who the Pharisees were, so that we can see more easily why they related to Jesus in the way they did. These technical sections are marked with a spade.

Important doctrines

The second kind of background section appears with passages which have important doctrines contained in them and which we need to study in more depth if we are to grow as Christians. Special sections that explain them to us are marked with a face as above.

Stop and look

This feature gives us the chance to stand back from the action and take stock. It gives a summary of what to look for in the passages we are about to read, and useful background material.

Stop and think

This feature appears with passages which highlight important themes or teaching. Bible references and questions will help you think them through. Write down your answers or use them as a framework for group discussion.

Turn on the light

An eye for the familiar

The London Eye, a huge Ferris wheel on the south bank of the Thames in London, transports its passengers way above the skyline of the British capital. The 'flight' starts at ground level and many familiar buildings such as the Houses of Parliament and Big Ben are viewed from the usual perspective. As the pod of the London Eye ascends, so the passenger gradually sees the London landmarks from a very different angle. Gradually soaring way above all the other buildings, familiar sights can then be viewed quite differently.

This is an illustration of how the epistles of John take a number of themes and look at them from a variety of perspectives. Throughout the letters John visits and revisits the themes of Jesus, light, love, sin, holiness, the Holy Spirit and the antichrists. Each time he returns to a topic it is as if the Ferris wheel has travelled a little higher and so the vantage point and the understanding is just a little clearer. Familiar teaching is reinforced and reapplied, so that the reader has more than one opportunity to grasp and marvel at the message being presented.

Who is John? Why did he write?

It is widely agreed that the same person, the Apostle John, wrote the Gospel of John and all three letters known as the epistles of John in the New Testament, although there are some who think that the letters might have been written by someone who was deliberately pretending to be the Apostle John, following his style and tone. The Apostle

John was, at the time these letters were written, in his old age and living in the area of Ephesus. He wrote to the congregations around Ephesus with whom he had a close relationship and about whom he was particularly concerned. The letters are likely to have been written around AD 90.

The term Apostle was used of those who travelled alongside Jesus for his three years of ministry. They were the original disciples, who heard him with their own ears, saw him with their own eyes and touched him for themselves (1 John 1:1). They had a particular role in establishing and leading the church in its early days. They were held in high esteem in the church as it grew and developed. John was one of the closest to Jesus, and in the Gospel of John he refers to himself as 'the disciple Jesus loved' (John 21:20, 24).

John had a particular concern in writing his letters. There are three main themes that he wants his readers to understand. The first theme is that of love. He returns to it time and time again. He has known the powerful effect of the love of Christ in his own life and in the life of communities that are committed to Christ. He is also aware of the damage that can be done when people claim to be Christians and yet don't show the love of Christ in their daily routines and relationships.

The second theme is that of false discipleship and false teaching. Many times John refers to those who deceived believers by claiming to be preaching a Christian gospel and yet, when their teaching is scrutinized, it is found that they deny Jesus Christ as both fully human and fully divine. Influenced by the Gnostics, who believed that the body and physical matter are evil, they taught that Jesus could not be fully divine because it would be anathema for God to take on a physical body when it is evil. They denied therefore that Jesus of Nazareth is the Christ, but taught that the spiritual Christ adopted the body of Jesus at his baptism until his death. This heresy had caused division and broken relationships within the church. It had no power to transform lives or develop a community of love and harmony.

The third theme that stands out amongst the many themes is that of sin. There are some marvellous words about confession and forgiveness. There are also strong words about admitting sin's existence and seeking not to sin.

CHILDREN OF GOD
LIVING IN THE
LIGHT

1 John 1:1 – 3:10

Stop and look

The authorship of the first letter of John is linked to the question of who wrote other documents thought of as John's. There are five books in the New Testament that Christian tradition ascribes to the Apostle John. They are the Gospel of John, the three letters of John and the book of Revelation. There is a similarity of language and teaching, issues and concerns in the five different writings. However, evidence about authorship of the letters is not conclusive.

It seems clear that the inspiration and traditions behind the five Johannine documents was John the Apostle, the beloved disciple himself. What is not so clear is how far the community around John the Apostle were involved in the writing of the letters or whether an elder or other leader wrote at least the second and third letters. What is reasonably certain is that the letters originated in an authentic apostolic context.

Some have thought that there was another 'John', John the elder, separate from John the Apostle, who might have been the author of 2 and 3 John. The letters are written from 'the elder' and some have taken this to mean that there is a second writer named John. However, if we accept the trustworthiness of early Christian tradition, which accepted the Apostle John as the author of the three letters, then it is not difficult to understand that the use of the term 'elder' was one adopted by the Apostle to express his seniority in years and experience.

Some have suggested that the letters were written from Syria, although it is more likely that the letters were addressed to Christian communities under the Apostle John's leadership, which centred around Ephesus. The first letter of John is generally thought to have been written around AD 80–90.

In the first part of our studies in the letters of John we see an appeal to the believers that they should not be misled by faulty ideas that destroy the heart of the Christian message. There were those claiming that the Son of God did not die since he is Spirit and could not die. John emphasizes that if Christ did not become truly human and die, then there is no Christian faith. John encourages those who know Jesus Christ to hold on to the faith and understanding that they had when they first believed.

1 John 1:1–4

An eyewitness

John launches straight into his theme of Jesus being the true Son of God.

There is nothing like the report of someone who was actually there to bring to life an event. Their words have weight and credibility because they have firsthand experience of what happened. As John begins his letter he starts with an eyewitness account of what he writes about. He was actually there, he saw Jesus, he knew him. So what he writes is not second-hand or passed-on insight, but he writes with an understanding and conviction of having been there and seen the man who is God, the Word of Life.

There is no formal greeting to begin the letter, as was the convention of the day. There is no 'Dear …' giving us the clue to whom the letter was written. Maybe John had an urgency to get his message across and did not want to waste words, when it was obvious to whom he was writing.

John uses all the force he can to make it known that God, the Word of life, has appeared amongst them. That

Word of life, Jesus Christ, is both a person and a message. Jesus cannot be separated from the message he brought; his personality – both fully God and fully human – is the living embodiment of God's message. It is this person that John has touched and known as a friend and a leader. There are links with the prologue of John's Gospel (John 1:1–18), where there is a much more detailed explanation of the Word becoming a person.

These opening verses are full of excitement and a sense of incredulity at all that the author has to tell. He writes of Jesus, who except for the time of his life here on earth, is outside of the constraints of time as we know it. He was from the beginning, at creation, with God the Father, as the eternal Word. Although he was there from the beginning, it is he that they have touched, listened to, seen, lived alongside and known. This is an amazing and astonishing message.

So crucial is the foundation that John is laying in these opening phrases, that you can almost feel the energy and emphasis with which he tries to persuade his readers of the truth of what he is writing. The Word of life is Jesus of Nazareth himself, God in human form before them. John could testify, in court if necessary, that Jesus the Word, who was with God the Father from the beginning, is the one who appeared to them. John is concerned because he doesn't want them to miss out on being partners in this incredible message. John doesn't want them to be distracted or diverted by misleading influences that have the appearance of the truth, but are in fact a denial of the truth.

John wants his readers to be reminded about the Word of life so that they might know the richness and the fullness of life that is only possible as a true believer. For the believer there is a deep relationship with God and with other Christians. The relationship with other believers consists of support and love and partnership in sharing the message of good news in Christ Jesus. When people have faith in God and in his Son then they can have friendship of the most fulfilling kind with others who share the faith.

His purpose in writing is declared in the last sentence of this section, that their pleasure and delight might be all that it could be. The author is concerned for both himself and his friends around Ephesus that he is writing to, that together they might know the full joy that God intended his followers to share. John wants to encourage and build up his readers so that they might know again the fulfilment they had when they first understood all that God in Christ meant to them. Circumstances, as we shall see later on, have undermined their confidence, their joy and their hope. This letter seeks to remind them of all that is basic to their community as God's people and to give them back the trust and expectation that they once knew.

There is great encouragement and joy when others are walking in the truth, and conversely great disappointment and sadness when people who once walked with the Lord have fallen away. To hear of someone who is tentative and hesitant in their faith going on with God and growing in their spiritual life is an inspiration to many others. We should probably encourage each other more often with testimonies and demonstrations of God at work in our lives, to build up those around us.

Questions

1. John, the author of this letter, was an eyewitness to the resurrection (John 20:3–8). How important is it for later generations of Christians to know that an eyewitness to the events of Jesus' life wrote the Gospel and the letters?
2. These verses remind us that Jesus was born in human flesh and was also fully God. What are your thoughts about God becoming human? How difficult is it for us to grasp the idea that God became human (the incarnation), that God with all his incredible power could come amongst the people of this world with all the weaknesses of human existence? Could God have saved us without becoming human?
3. John wrote his letter to support and encourage those he

wrote to. Have you ever received a letter or telephone call that has been a spiritual help to you? What did you especially value about it? Could you, or your group, communicate 'joy' (verse 4) to someone right now?

1 John 1:5–7

Light and darkness

Knowing that Jesus is the Son of God is like living in the light and seeing things as they really are. Living without knowledge of Jesus is like living in darkness and in ignorance of the truth.

John began, in the opening verses of this letter, by reminding his readers of Jesus, the Word of life, who is the basis of their relationships and joy together. In these verses he explains further what this means as he focuses on God, the Father of Jesus, the Word. John asserts that God is without any smudge or stain on his character. He emphasizes that there is a quality of transparency about God found in no other being. God is pure and his power is holy. These verses (5b–7) are a summary of the message of salvation; they are the gospel in a nutshell.

Since God is light, then in God there is no darkness. Darkness and light cannot coexist; if you have one, by mutual exclusion you cannot have the other. One expels the other. We are so used to every person, institution and organization that we come across having flaws of some kind. For God to be light, to be flawless and perfect in love and holiness, is something we need to absorb and learn from and seek to imitate. God is without blemish. He has no history that he needs to hide, no skeletons in the cupboard. God is light and so we can rely on his word, his actions and his promises.

Just as light expels the darkness, as illumination in a room forces out the shadows and gloom, similarly God drives out evil and sin. His presence sends evil away. God is repelled by darkness such as hatred and indifference, rebellion and pride. It is therefore a nonsense for someone to claim to be a Christian, a follower of Jesus Christ, and yet happily to behave in a way dishonouring to God. God could not be in relationship with such a person. It would be a denial of his character. Walking in the light is to do with walking in openness to God, while walking in darkness is walking with all the windows to God closed.

John points out the contradiction of a believer claiming to be in a close relationship with God while living a wilfully sinful life. To live in darkness means a person cannot be living in a close relationship with God, because God is repelled by the darkness. God cannot exist with evil and sin, so he cannot be in communion with a person who is wantonly disobedient and willingly living in darkness. John has in mind those who are living a life of deceit, who are claiming to be holy and yet living a life of unholiness, not those who are struggling with sin and know they need God's help.

These words are a reminder that it is not enough to sing all the latest worship songs, claim great spiritual experiences from God and testify to the Holy Spirit being powerfully at work, if at the same time people are dishonest in their business or at work, immoral in their sexual relationships, or proud and greedy in their dealings with others. John is emphasizing that God's people must 'walk the talk'; they cannot have a relationship with God and be walking in the light if they are not seeking to deal with issues of ungodliness in their lives. There is a requirement for a follower of Jesus Christ to be a person of integrity. Their words and actions should be in harmony; worship and church life should be consistent with their personal behaviour and activity outside of church. God cannot be in fellowship and at work in those who have spiritual split personalities.

There is a danger that in our caring, indulgent, postmodern world, Christian communities may be lenient on wrongdoing. It is easy to take a soft approach to sin, which is not biblical, and is far from what John is teaching in these verses. Wrongdoing is somehow excused as an addiction or genetic predisposition, but the Bible describes it as rebellion and disobedience against God.

If a person is involved in behaviour that they know to be contrary to biblical teaching and they pretend that it doesn't matter, then they are living a lie; they are not living by the truth of God's word. They are dishonouring God and his name and causing him deep sadness. They are destroying or at least spiritually disabling themselves. It is not possible to know the full joy and pleasure of God's life while living wilfully in sin.

A believer who walks in the light of God's life in Christ and seeks to live in dependence on the Holy Spirit will be transformed. The power of God at work in them and other believers will mean that there will be no barriers dividing them from others, and fellowship with other Christians will be genuine and satisfying. It is sin and darkness that divide and destroy relationships. It is light and love that draw people together and bring deep relationships of trust and care.

The work of Jesus on the cross, when his blood flowed on behalf of all who have sinned, means that, daily, believers can be cleansed before God from the spiritual effects of their wrongdoing and they can have good relationships together because they are united in Christ.

Questions

1. Since these verses summarize the gospel message, use them to make a list of the main points of the gospel. Discuss how to communicate these points to non-believers.

2. Do you have to be perfect to walk in the light 'with windows open to God'? Compile a checklist of the qualities needed to walk in the light with 'windows open to God'.
3. Is your country or society a darker place spiritually in the twenty-first century than in previous centuries?

Sinlessness and sanctification

Down the centuries there have been those who have claimed to have reached a state of total sinlessness. Known as the Holiness Movement, there are those who believe that as Christians we should reach a place where we are without sin. We should reach a state where God's Holy Spirit has so worked in us that we are sanctified and without blemish or wrongdoing before God.

For instance, John Wesley, the founder of Methodism, taught that Christians could become perfect by receiving a second blessing of holiness. Keeping the blessing required effort and commitment, but this was possible through devotion and the Spirit's help. The believer who had achieved a state of holiness could make mistakes and errors through misjudgment or ignorance, but their intention remained sinless and therefore sanctified.

John in his letter makes it clear that if we claim to be without sin then we are misguided (1 John 1:8). While the Holiness Movement is to be commended for setting high standards and encouraging individuals to be pure in all they do, it does not seem to be consistent with biblical truth when it claims that a state of sinlessness is possible in this life. The old nature too readily battles against the Christian's determination to be perfect.

We can understand from Paul's own battle with sin that this was a problem for even the Apostles (Romans 7:14–20). Paul genuinely and sincerely wished to do what is right and to be holy, but he found that it was impossible.

His old nature, the law of sin, was still at work in him, preventing him being perfect and holy. One day when our sinful natures are completely changed we will be holy in every way, but until that time we have to accept that sin is a frustrating part of our lives.

Walking in the light is not sinless perfection, but rather living in constant repentance and forgiveness. Later in this letter (1 John 3:6–9) the theme of sinless living is addressed again. There is a reminder that, although our sin is always evident in our lives, it should not be something which the believer indulges in or accepts, but something that is resisted and for which daily renewal and forgiveness is sought.

Stop and think: Light

The term light is used frequently throughout the Bible to illustrate God's character and activities. Most consistently, light is used to symbolize the saving presence of God in the world, and darkness is a sign of sin or the absence of God in a person's life or in a situation (see John 12:35–36).

Other uses of light to illustrate God's character

- God's purity – Isaiah 5:20
- God's glory – 1 Timothy 6:15–16
- God's word as it brings understanding – Psalm 119:105
- God's favour – Psalm 4:6
- God's knowledge – Psalm 139:11–12
- God's unchanging nature – James 1:17

Which of these qualities most encourages you? Discuss why light is a helpful image for understanding God.

In John's writings, both in his Gospel and this first letter, he makes frequent use of light to express his thoughts about God and walking in his ways. In John 8:12 Jesus describes himself as 'the light of the world'. This is one among many metaphors for the work of God in Christ. The darkness of the world is seen in a variety of ways: poverty, loneliness, hatred, violence, greed and injustice, to name just a few. All of these have resulted from the broken relationship between God and humanity, which meant that sin rules the lives of all people.

God's remedy for healing the broken relationship between himself and the people he created was to send Jesus as the Light who would dispel the darkness and make an open relationship between himself and his people possible again.

▶ Consider the ways in which Christian action brings light into your community.

▶ What are the greatest areas of darkness in our world? Compare the darkness of poverty and deprivation and the darkness of wealth and success.

▶ How might the use of light be a helpful feature in worship, either in a small group or individually? Seek to use light in a creative way to worship God either on your own or in your group.

1 John 1:8 – 2:2

Don't deny sin

John tackles the problem of sin head on, showing its relevance to all, including believers.

These are some of the most powerful pastoral words in the Bible. For the arrogant and proud they are a rebuke. For the ashamed and humiliated they bring comfort and hope. These words give clear insight into how God's people should view and deal with their sin. It is an important issue, and one of the concerns for the present growing global culture is that the focus on tolerance and understanding leads to a trivializing of the importance of sin.

John is simple and clear in his message. There are those in the communities that he is writing to who are claiming to be without sin – claiming that they have come to a point of such spirituality that they have left sin behind. John teaches that this is not possible. He says in effect, 'don't be so stupid as to deny that you have sin'. 'My sin is always before me' (Psalm 51:3) is the perspective John encourages his readers to take.

If we have an ounce of honesty and reflect for even a second, we will acknowledge that sin is always a struggle and a battle. It was for Paul, who said, 'I have the desire to do what is good, but I cannot carry it out' (Romans 7:18), and so it is for every person except Jesus himself. If we imagine that we are without sin then we are only fooling ourselves. Everyone else can see it. If you have any doubt, ask someone what your weaknesses are; they will soon tell you. If we are deceiving ourselves in such a way as to think that we have no sin then the Holy Spirit cannot be in us; otherwise he would have led us into an understanding of our flaws before God.

The second point that John is keen to emphasize is that we should regularly confess all the things that we do wrong: the thoughts, the attitudes, the words, as well as the actions. The old saints used to say 'keep a short account with God'. In other words, don't put yourself in the situation where there is a long list of unconfessed sins which have not been brought to God. Don't think that some sins don't matter: 'It may be just a little thought, but watch your little thoughts, they become words. Your words become actions, your actions become habits and your habits become character. Watch your character because it becomes your destiny' (Words of Wisdom internet site).

God is patient and is always generously disposed towards us. If we admit our weaknesses and failings he not only forgives us, but also acts as a spiritual washing powder. Like the biological powders that dissolve the ground-in dirt and grime, the grease and stains, so God removes the spiritual filth from our lives.

In the final verse of this chapter John argues with passion the total contradiction of thinking we have no sin or thinking that somehow our attitudes and our use of words, our behaviour and habits are not sinful. If we hold to this view then we make God into a liar, because God speaks clearly of the human heart being 'deceitful above all things' (Jeremiah 17:9).

I wonder what your impression is of the writers of the New Testament. It is easy to overlook the fact that these are real flesh-and-blood authors, with feelings and a genuine relationship with the people to whom they write. In 2:1 we begin to understand how deeply John feels for those to whom he is writing. 'My dear children' is an affectionate term showing a fatherly concern for those for whom he has responsibility under God. As a godly father he wants them to be the best that they can be. His purpose in writing is to help them avoid sin if at all possible. However, he is realistic and aware of human weakness.

John sets the highest standards. He hopes that believers might avoid sin altogether but, knowing that isn't possible, he doesn't want them to be defeated by their failure. He seeks to reassure them that when they do sin they have a saviour who is also a defence lawyer: Jesus Christ, the one in whom there is no sin.

The irony is plain. The one who is sinless is the one who speaks in defence of those who do sin. Jesus Christ is the most persuasive advocate because he is without blemish, he is righteous. A testimony on behalf of a defendant by someone of good character is persuasive, but to be defended by the Son of God himself, who is without wrongdoing of any kind, is incredible. To be represented by such an intermediary is awesome.

The Righteous One (2:1) is a title applied to Christ as the only person who has lived his life without sin. Jesus lived on earth for thirty-three years and never gave into temptation, did not live selfishly, and was without pride and arrogance. Such purity of character is not possible for those born into sin.

Jesus Christ's defence of his people is effective because he is the solution to the problem of sin. God looks at the sin of humankind and is repelled by it; the absence of holiness and the depravity he sees is inexcusable. Jesus Christ, however, is there as the defence; he points his Father to his own death as a sacrifice, taking the punishment for humanity's sin. The death of Christ paid the price and took the punishment for all the sin and wrongdoing of the whole world.

There are so many key verses in John's epistles, but verse 2 is crucial for making sure that we understand the significance of the cross. The death of Christ is central to salvation and faith. Without the death of Christ on the cross there can be no forgiveness of sins, no salvation, no eternal life and no relationship with God.

The death of Christ is an 'atoning sacrifice'. In other words, it is Christ surrendering his life as an innocent victim, taking the punishment due to humankind for breaking the law. When people sin they have broken the law of God. God knew he could not save his people without the problem of sin being dealt with, so he sent his own perfect son to give up his life, to take the punishment for the sin of the world. All people are, therefore, in God's debt; his generosity in sending his son can never be matched by anything anyone might try to do for him.

John is not saying in verse 2 that all will be saved, a misconstruction some have put on the words 'also for the sins of the whole world'. The atoning sacrifice is sufficient to take the punishment for the sins of the whole world, but it still leaves open the need for the response of the individual to the offer of salvation.

It is easy in the contemporary world to go a bit soft on sin. It's not a word that enters into our everyday language. We have expunged the terms 'living in sin' or 'leading a sinful life' as somehow too judgmental and intolerant for our open-minded communities. However, John's focus on sin is a good reminder that our wrongdoing and disobedience to God matter; sin is serious and of the greatest concern. These verses might make us reflect on all the aspects of our life that are not what God wants: those attitudes that are proud, selfish or arrogant, the behaviour that is inconsiderate or disobedient. If only we were as concerned about our sin as God is.

Questions

1. Are there ways in which as Christians we deceive ourselves by overlooking sin in our lives? Are we too 'soft on sin' both in others and ourselves? Read Psalm 51:1–12 together as a prayer of confession. Confess your sins to God and if possible before each other, and pray for each other that God's grace may bring light and holiness into your lives. Write your sins on a small piece of paper and then burn them to symbolize 1 John 1:9.
2. Has the church become too accommodating to people in their lax moral and spiritual behaviour, and does it fail to challenge sinful behaviour? How should it do this?

3. What might we conclude about those who deny the importance of sin and are indifferent to the consequences of sin in their lives (1:6, 8, 10)? Pray together for those among your acquaintances who consider the concept of sin an irrelevancy to them.
4. Why do different cultures regard certain types of sin as more or less serious than we do (for example, drinking alcohol, polygamy, respect for elders)? What does this tell us about our own blindness or oversensitivity?

Christ the atoning sacrifice

Some of the technical words of the New Testament, such as 'atoning sacrifice' or 'atonement', would have been much easier for the first-century Christians to understand than they are for us. Atoning would have been a familiar idea in a world where animal sacrifice was common. Such practices are much less common in today's world and the word atonement is rarely used, so we are left floundering by the words used by the New Testament writers. Yet many of these seemingly difficult concepts are straightforward if we understand the background to them.

Jewish Christians would have immediately understood 'atoning sacrifice'. Greek Christians would have understood the imagery of sacrifice and making an offering for wrongdoing. Atonement is about putting right a relationship that has gone wrong because of failure or error. When damage has been done to a relationship then there is a price to pay to mend the relationship. The price paid is the atoning sacrifice.

To make an atoning sacrifice therefore means to make a sacrificial offering so that a broken relationship can be restored. At a simple level, if someone I know damages my car they may offer to pay the costs of repair so that the relationship we have is not broken by the damage they have done. In a much greater way the relationship between God and his people has been broken by the wrongdoing of the human race, which we call sin. In order for the relationship between God and his people to be mended a sacrificial offering has to be made to pay the price of sin.

Sin cuts people off from God because God is holy and cannot have anything to do with sin. God has an aversion to all that is not pure. Everyone sins, as all are born into sin, so the problem of sin is universal. Sin provokes God's righteous and just anger because whatever form the sin takes, it is damaging to the community God created. People cannot atone for their own sin because they cannot make an adequate offering. No efforts that anyone makes can ever be enough. Sin is so serious that only the death of a perfect person is adequate.

The initiative in healing the broken relationship and bringing about atonement comes from God's generous nature and his desire to forgive rather than punish his people. He offers his own son, which is a reflection of his incredible love, for the people he created. While people had no idea of the terrible state they were in, separated from God and unable to do anything about it, God's love prompted him to make atonement possible through Jesus Christ.

Under the old covenant, declared to Moses, temporary atonement was received through the sacrifices of animals. Those who sinned offered animals as a substitute for themselves, so that God's punishment and anger went on the animal rather than on the Israelite. Under the new covenant Jesus is the high priest who offers the sacrifice as well as being the sacrifice, a sacrifice which is effective for everyone for all time.

There are many images that convey the rich depth of meaning of atonement. Most obviously it is the forgiveness of sins; since the punishment for our sin has been taken by Jesus Christ, then we can receive forgiveness. Atonement is also understood to be cleansing and purification. Sin makes each person impure, contaminated and dirty before God. Through the sacrifice of Christ, his blood takes away all the dirt and mess of our lives and makes us clean before God. It is also reconciliation and the healing of the broken relationship with God. Rather than coming to God in fear and seeing him only as a judge whose verdict upon us is death, we come to God as Abba, Father, one who is our friend and comforter. Atonement is God redeeming or buying back his people, like a slave having his freedom bought. Without Christ we are enslaved to sin, unable to help ourselves. Christ has paid the price of our freedom with his own life. Finally, atonement makes the believer holy as they come into a close relationship with God and are filled with his Holy Spirit.

Atonement is 'at-one-ment': it is to be made at one with God, from whom we are separated because of sin.

Other important New Testament passages on atonement include John 6:51–58, Romans 3:21–26 and 5:1–11, and Hebrews 10:1–14.

1 John 2:3–11

Walking in the light

Being a Christian is not simply a matter of words and accepting certain beliefs; it is obedience to the teaching and commands of Christ.

True knowledge (verses 3–6)

I don't think people who claim that the Bible is an out-of-date book can ever have read it properly. There are parts of the Bible that take a bit of effort to understand, and it may take some perseverance to grasp the context and background of some passages. Despite that, the Bible is amazingly contemporary in its relevance.

The verses we are now studying fall into this category. They are so practical and applicable to us today. How can you tell if someone is a believer? The answer John gives is another question: are they living as a believer and following the teaching and example of Jesus? A simple test, but one that is not so simple to apply in practice. For example, someone who has become a Christian from a background of alcohol and drug abuse, loose family relationships and routine dishonesty may have more difficulty living according to the values of Christ than someone brought up in a Christian environment. However, there should be evidence of the intention to live according to Biblical principles. We know someone has become a Christian when there is a difference in the way they live and a desire to submit to the leading of Christ.

John states what is logical. Those who declare they are Christians and profess to know God should affirm it in their behaviour. If they do not follow the teaching and commands of Christ then they are living dishonestly and the Spirit of God, who is the Spirit of truth, cannot be in them. John wrote these words to counter those who claimed to be Christians and yet denied the teaching of Christ about himself. As we will see later in the letter, they denied that Jesus was divine or that it was the Son of God who was crucified. They taught that God could not suffer in the body since the body was evil. They proclaimed that suffering, obedience and purity of the body were insignificant. They denied the central characteristic of true faith, that it is lived out in the physical body, which can involve suffering and requires self-control.

It is a curious idea for us today that people would claim to be a Christian and claim to have the Spirit of God in them when they have not. In our liberal, secular society it is difficult to imagine that anyone would claim a relationship with God through Christ unless they genuinely had such a relationship. However, for strange and bizarre reasons individuals may seek to convince others of their faith when they do not have an authentic trust and relationship with God. There are examples of leaders of cults who manipulate and control others. Often on the surface their claims are plausible, but scrutiny of their behaviour brings serious concerns. Such concerns may be linked to dubious sexual ethics, financial corruption, unhealthy relationships or an unwillingness to be accountable to others.

For a whole host of reasons there are those who claim to know God through Jesus Christ and yet do not know him. Their false claims are exposed in the long term by their behaviour and relationships with others. When someone knows God through Christ then their behaviour will be in harmony with the teaching of Christ. When someone pretends to know God through Christ, after a while the hollowness of their claim becomes apparent.

Every so often we learn from the newspapers or television news of a Christian leader who, having made all kinds of claims about knowing God and being true to their message, are discovered to be something quite different. These words urge us to be wise and cautious when we hear comments that are not consistent with the message of Jesus Christ, and to be careful if someone makes great claims of spiritual maturity when their behaviour suggests otherwise.

In verse 5 John goes on to much more positive and encouraging thoughts. When a believer follows the teaching of Jesus and obeys all his commands, then that person not only shows love for God but God's love enables that person to be all that God wants him or her to be.

At the time this letter was written, the Gospels or parts of the Gospel material would have been circulating on scrolls of parchment. In the different Christian communities spread around the Mediterranean, believers would have read together the recorded words of Christ and the facts of his ministry as chronicled by the Gospel writers. The believers would have known that what was required of them was to follow the teaching of Christ about God and his kingdom and all the practical instruction on how disciples of Christ should behave and the character they should aspire to.

To 'walk as Jesus did' that John sets down is to live a life of service to God, suffering for the kingdom, a willingness to give up what we might naturally find comfortable and easy, and live a life of holiness. The motivation for this extraordinary way of life is love for God and love from God. It is only with his help that we can live as Jesus did, both in our behaviour and our character. It seems that so many in our world, especially in comfortable and materialistic Western cultures, find it difficult to relate to such selfless teaching. And yet God by his Holy Spirit does work within us when we allow him.

I recently spoke to a young woman of twenty three: attractive and well educated, with the personality and skills to be successful in the business and commercial world. She has heard the voice of God calling her to live selflessly. She would like the car, the clothes, the boyfriends, the social life that her contemporaries have. But a stronger conviction is that she wants to serve God. She wants to follow God's leading to care for abandoned children and show them the love of Christ. She is prepared to give up many of the comforts and opportunities so many of us take for granted. She knows that she may face suffering and difficulties that will be hard, but she is determined to walk as Jesus did and do as John encourages all of us to do.

There had been disruptions and difficulties in the lives of the Christian communities to whom John writes. False teachers had said things about Christ that had confused and misled the fellowships. They had caused division and poor relationships, and had destroyed the love and unity of the believers. John writes to these Christians to heal their wounds now that the false teachers have left. He wants them to regain their confidence and hope and the depth of relationships that they can have in Christ.

Similar circumstances occur today when church communities go through painful and sad disruptions caused by wrong teaching or overenthusiastic and insensitive personalities. When Christian communities go through tough times they need to be soothed, taught soundly and encouraged back to the place of confidence and love in Christ.

43

The old truth newly expressed (verses 7–11)

John moves from calling them children (2:1) to addressing them as friends. He reflects the multidimensional nature of the bond they have. He feels like a father to them, but he also sees them as friends. There are times when we need to be cared for and cosseted like children, but more often we need friends. We need to be treated as an equal, able both to give and to receive. In a good relationship those involved will be able to respond as the circumstances need and dictate. Usually in a relationship there is mutual respect. At times of stress or difficulty it may be necessary for one in the relationship to be the parent and one to receive help as a child. However, if the relationship is always like this, it is unlikely that the individual being treated and responding as a child will develop fully in Christ, with the maturity that God wants for us.

John makes it plain that he is not adding anything new to the teaching they have already received. The gospel they heard from Jesus himself, which they had from the beginning, has not changed. The original teaching of Jesus is the same command as they are hearing now. It is the same message of God's grace and forgiveness, the same message of their need of a Saviour and their hope found in the Messiah.

Having stated that there is nothing new, John now points out that, although it is the old command, the emphasis that he is putting on it is new. The command is new because they have moved on as a Christian community and understand more fully what it means to walk in the light. The difficult experiences they have been through have made them more aware of what it means to allow the truth of Christ to affect every aspect of their lives.

When Jesus came as the light of the world, he came, amongst other things, to heal relationships. John emphasizes this aspect of living in the light, the reconciling power of God's love through Christ to create deep relationships. To live in the light involves loving our brothers and sisters in Christ. If there is hatred in our heart for God's people then we are not living in the light but are still stumbling around in the darkness. Again John points out how illogical some of our claims are. We cannot claim to walk in the light with Jesus as our Lord and hate a brother or sister. If we do hate a brother or sister then that indicates we are living in darkness and have not understood how the light should transform every aspect of our lives.

Those who are not in a good relationship with brothers and sisters in the fellowship are stumbling around in the darkness, even though they don't realize it. How many in our churches are clinging to bitterness and anger against a brother or sister in Christ for differences that occurred years ago? John reminds us that such behaviour is evidence of being in darkness and is not the behaviour of those who belong to the kingdom of God. It is all too easy for the darkness to blind us to the error of our ways. We so easily justify and excuse our resentment of and hostility to others in the fellowship of God's people. We should be repenting of these things. It should be a characteristic of God's people that they are united and in harmony with each other.

These words are a reminder to those in leadership and anyone who takes the name of Christ to find ways to work with others even when there are disagreements. So often it is at a leadership level that differences and animosity are most evident and most damaging. The arrogant manner in which some have thought they were 'doing God's will' has caused concern about whether they are walking in the light at all.

Questions

1. Discuss ways in which the church down the centuries has claimed to know God and claimed to be living by the truth when in fact its actions are not consistent with the truth and it is in fact lying? How can we avoid such error in ourselves?
2. Why does personal obedience to the commands of

Christ seem so difficult, particularly with reference to hating a brother or sister in Christ?

3. Many people would find it difficult to accept that the commands of Jesus should be followed. How would you answer someone who argues that there is no such thing as 'the truth' and that whatever someone believes is truth for them?

4. How can churches express this kind of love (verse 7) for 'brothers and sisters' across national, tribal and cultural boundaries? Think of practical responses.

1 John 2:12–17

The family and the world

Being in the family of God gives confidence to every member, from the youngest to the oldest. Each one has been forgiven and has overcome the evil one, so now they need to ensure they don't put anyone or anything in the place of God.

At this point in his letter John wants to make his appeal and his writing as personal and as intimately appropriate as possible. His pastoral heart is clear as he writes to build up and to encourage, not to rebuke. He builds on the fact that their sins have been forgiven. The difficult things he has had to say about them claiming not to sin (1:8–10) are said, and now he is on easier ground as he affirms them in their faith and their forgiveness.

John seeks to be inclusive. He refers to children, fathers and young people. He presents them with the clear message that the light of the world has come and the light that Jesus offers is for everyone. The hearers might receive and apply that message in different ways; it may be that different aspects of the Word of life apply in different ways in their lives. Despite that, it is a message for all.

The poetry of these verses repeat and emphasize the themes of knowing the Father, overcoming the evil one, and forgiveness. The readers of the letter have been forgiven only because of Christ and his sacrifice on the cross. This has led to them knowing the Father, the one who is from the beginning. In the forgiveness they have received they have known the Father, begun to understand his purposes and plans, and grasped his character and kindness to them.

Through the power of the Holy Spirit the believers have received forgiveness and come to know the Father and have therefore defeated the power of darkness in their lives. Living in the light is a spiritual battle that involves defeating powers of darkness. By becoming Christians the believers have won the war with Satan in their lives; there are still battles to be fought, but they are skirmishes with an enemy who is defeated but has yet to give up the fight.

It seems as if John can hardly contain his enthusiasm and excitement in these verses. He is so pleased and delighted that his friends, those he looks on as family, know the Father, have been conquerors over Satan and have received forgiveness for their sins. He concludes this poetic interlude with a comment to the young people, who are always so precious to a community as they, more than most, represent the future. John is encouraged because the young people are strong; they have faith that will persevere, that doesn't give up at the slightest difficulty. John knows this because he sees the Word of God living in them. They have taken seriously their relationship with Jesus Christ and are behaving in a way that is evidence of God at work in their lives.

These words remind the battered and bruised Christians to whom John writes of the truths that are their foundation and anchor. When tough situations arise, those without a strong basis of faith and a firm trust in God and the gospel message can easily be discouraged and undermined. Similarly today when challenging circumstances

face us, we need to remind ourselves of our past understanding and experiences of God. We need to cling to the
truth of all that we have known and learnt in Christ and
the battles we have fought and won in his strength. We
can then be confident in God, who holds us through every
circumstance. It is good to be people of faith who remain
constant in hope whatever the situation rather than
people of uncertainty who panic the moment circumstances are difficult.

John moves on, in verses 15–17, to thoughts that at first
sight are difficult to accept and grasp, yet alone apply. We
are told not to love the world or anything in the world and
we immediately think that there is so much in the world
around us that is beautiful and appealing – music, nature,
art, literature, the wonder of science or mathematics. How
then are we to understand these verses that command us
in a direct and uncompromising manner not to love the
world?

What John is encouraging his readers, and therefore us,
to do is to have everything in the right perspective. Put
God at the centre and allow all these other aspects of the
world to be seen in the light of God's grace and sover-
eignty. We should not love the world; in other words, we
should not make an idol of or give undue value to the
things of this world. There may be many aspects of this
world that are loveable, that we appreciate and are grateful for, but only God should take that central place and is
worthy of our adoration and worship, our praise and
devotion. Love of family and friends, brothers and sisters
in Christ, should develop from our love of God himself.
God cannot share his glory with another (Isaiah 42:8). It is
not possible to love God and give him the priority in our
lives that is his due, and also give the same significance to
something else.

John urges us not to be tempted to put something or
someone else in the place of God. If we are committed to
something in the world to such an extent that we cannot
live without it or we refuse to give it up, then it is likely
that we have fallen into the trap of loving the world. In so

doing we have excluded the love of the Father from our lives.

Worldliness used to be an idea that was widely talked about in the church. There were a whole list of pursuits and vocations that were regarded as worldly and that 'good' Christians did not engage in. Such categorizing of activities was rarely helpful and resulted in an approach to spirituality that was defined in negative terms. It was therefore not holy to go to the cinema or to drink alcohol, to wear make-up or to dance. Holiness and spirituality are of course positive qualities that were sadly misrepresented in this negative categorizing of activities. Thankfully such an approach to Christian lifestyle is largely a thing of the past; however, in leaving behind the language of 'worldliness' we have opened ourselves to the possibility of something far worse. Without the clear emphasis on worldliness there once was, we are in danger of being unwittingly trapped. Materialism, consumerism and the success culture, for example, which are not necessarily intrinsically evil, can become idols in our lives if we are not careful. Too easily we absorb the values and attitudes of the world around us rather than being centred on Christ.

John contrasts the kingdom of God with the world, the world being any aspect of creation and life that is not submitted to the lordship of Christ. John develops his thinking further by giving examples of what he means. By the cravings of people I am sure he has in mind the basic hankering for money, power and physical pleasures. No-one needs to look very far to discover that in every generation and in every century people have sold their souls for financial gain, for control over others and for hedonistic pleasures that bring only short-lived satisfaction. These hankerings and cravings John describes as passions or lusts, for that is what they can turn into, and then that leads to bragging and arrogance, which is far removed from the character and values of our heavenly Father.

The final verse of this section is a reminder that these things that seem so appealing and so attractive are transient and temporary. It is doing God's will that has value of a more permanent nature. Being in God's will and loving him above all others is significant for eternity. Many of us who have been Christians for years will affirm what John is writing in these verses, and yet that doesn't mean to say that it is easy to follow. Many a Christian leader or gifted disciple has fallen because the attraction of the world is so magnetic. We would be wise not to move away from these verses too quickly and to take time to consider what aspects of the world attract or tempt us most and could be the trap that snares us.

Questions

1. John focuses on children and young people in verses 12–14, encouraging them and giving them confidence. What more can we do in our Christian communities to build up and to give confidence and spiritual responsibility to the younger members?
2. What are the attractions of the world that most appeal to us? How do we resist the temptation to let such attractions take God's place in our lives?
3. How can we distinguish a spiritually healthy pursuit of money, music or sport from a spiritually unhealthy pursuit of such activities? Is it always easy to tell the difference between spiritually healthy motivation and destructive activities?
4. John mentions the world, the flesh and the devil in these verses (cf. Ephesians 2:1–3). How do these powers of evil interact with each other – and how do we combat them?

1 John 2:18–23

The antichrists and the last hour

False teachers who are antichrists have been stirring up trouble in the Christian community. John exposes them as the liars they are.

There is a lot of popular interest in anything even slightly connected with the end of the world. The theme of the antichrist attracts interest and excitement, particularly amongst those with an appetite for the sensational. It is therefore with a note of caution that we move forward in our study of John's epistle. Not because I wish to dampen anyone's enthusiasm or interest in God's word, but because I would warn that what is sometimes presented in a popular format as sensational, spectacular and a good topic for films and books is not necessarily the message that is intended.

The author refers to the time when he is writing as being 'the last hour'. This phraseology needs some explaining. The early Christians, those living in the first century, were convinced that Jesus would return within their lifetime, although Jesus himself never claimed this. When we read 'the last hour' in the New Testament it can have a sense of imminence about it and may lead to an expectation that the time for Jesus' return is within months or years and is about to happen. To have had to wait centuries and even two millennia is a surprise to those who have understood this to be a reference to literal time.

'The last hour' is a reference to the final days, the days between the ascension of Jesus and his return, which could be at any time. For believers this is a time of waiting.

God's purposes are being fulfilled, and during this time many would come with false teaching, whom John refers to as being 'antichrists'. The antichrists are those who do not have the kingdom of God as their focus, but who seek their own purposes.

The word 'antichrist' conjures up images of evil and destructive power, often from the realm of fantasy literature or horror films. Depictions of a beast or horned tyrant adapted from Revelation are some of the images that come to mind when we think about the antichrist. These unhelpful images make it harder for us to understand the grave danger that less fantastic characters, but with just as wicked personalities, hold for us. John calls antichrists those who come pretending to be from God and claiming to have the gospel message who are in fact charlatans and impostors.

The message they deliver does not result in the transforming power of the gospel in people's lives, but only brings division and discord. It appears from John's writing, both in this letter and in Revelation, that before the antichrist there are many forerunners who are referred to as 'the antichrists'. These are people who do not have the same degree of power and destructive intentions as the antichrist, but who have the imprint of Satan on them and the same intention to destroy the work of God in Christ amongst his people.

These false teachers stirred up controversy, caused rifts and then left to go elsewhere. It is interesting that John viewed the departure of these people as confirmation that they never really belonged. He is suggesting that if they had been authentic members of the body of Christ, then they would have continued to work out the issues and find reconciliation and life together in Christ. I am not quite sure what that says about our mobile communities today, and the number of people who move to another church as soon as there is something they don't quite agree with. The issues are complex and some move for godly reasons, but others maybe never were part of the community, never saw themselves as belonging, and so moved on easily without ever taking responsibility for their actions or words.

John is quick to affirm his readers (verse 20). He is keen to separate them from the antichrists and makes it clear that he is in no doubt that they are God's people. He knows they are because he recognizes the anointing of God in their lives and the work of the Holy Spirit amongst them. He is at pains to make clear to them that he is not writing because he has any doubts about their understanding or salvation, but to ensure that the truth is endorsed amongst them.

With his exquisite logic, John shows how clear the situation is. These people, spreading false teaching, are not of the truth because no lie comes from the truth; since they are spreading half-truths and untruths, they cannot be of the truth.

In verses 22–23 John gets to the heart of the problem of the teaching of the antichrists. They denied the full relationship between God and his Son. They taught that Jesus was not the fully divine Messiah, but a man whom God used. They were teaching the Docetic heresy. Docetism claims that Jesus was just a man and God clothed him with divinity to make him the Messiah, but he was never fully God in the form of a person. Biblical Christian belief is that Jesus was fully human and fully divine. He was not a man who had 'godliness' clothed around him, for that would have made him an inadequate Messiah.

The false teachers had arrived amongst the community of believers and arrogantly and without love or humility shared their erroneous views, causing division and improper behaviour, and leading to confusion and doubt. The person who makes such a denial, denying the relationship between Father and Son, cannot have the Father or they would know they were wrong. Anyone who denies the full divine nature of the Son cannot have any part with the Father because Father and Son are one, in an indivisible unity. To affirm the Son is to embrace the Father; not to acknowledge the Son in his full deity is to reject the Father.

These verses are a reminder of how easy it is to be

distracted from the truth. They also repeat the lesson that there are many who would wish to divert believers from their faith. These distracting and diversionary tactics by those who appear convincing and plausible are all part of the schemes and plans of the evil one.

Those who would divert God's people from the truth today come in many differing guises. There are those who brings us half-truths packaged to look like the whole truth, therefore misleading us and being dishonest in the message they convey. Current issues might include prosperity teaching, encouraging believers to think that God's blessing includes a guarantee of material prosperity if we pray and obey his leading, or teaching on healing that says that all should be physically healed or that God never intended his people to suffer. Many today on the more liberal wing of the church, while claiming to be Christians, would question the role and deity of Christ. This is a timely reminder that God's people should be on their guard and must protect the precious truth of the gospel from any and every misrepresentation.

John's argument is sensible. In a close family father and son are loyal and committed to each other. They will defend and protect each other. If one is not acceptable somewhere, then the other will not go there out of respect and love. Those who wish to be friends with the family cannot chose to have a relationship with one member and not the other. This is what John is contending. To be a Christian means to accept God, both Father and Son, fully. Believers cannot pick and choose which bits of doctrine they are comfortable with and which they would like to reject. Father, Son and Holy Spirit come as one, and to deny one is to deny them all.

Questions

1. What false teaching have you come across in your Christian experience? Often it takes the form of one doctrine, such as holiness or the Holy Spirit, which is

exaggerated and so becomes a falsehood. What damage has this teaching done in the lives of believers?

2. Why is there so much interest in the theme of the antichrist in horror films and in Christian teaching? What does this tell us about our society and our Christian values?

3. When someone claims to be teaching Christian truth and you are unsure about what they are saying, how can you deal with the situation constructively? More broadly, how can 'the truth' be safeguarded in the church of Jesus Christ?

 Stop and think: The antichrist

The latest candidate for the antichrist is Prince Charles. Apparently His Royal Highness gives the game away on his coat of arms, which features a kind of leopard, kind of bear feet and the mouth of the lion; according to some, this makes him the beast of Revelation 13:2. Add to this the fact that, as the eighth Charles, by some obscure calculation he matches the predictions of Revelation 17:9–11 that the beast will be the eighth in line. The clincher is when you add up the numerical values of the letters 'Prince of Wales', the total is 666 (cf. Revelation 13:18).

This is not a helpful way to understand Scripture. Every generation has viewed an enemy of some sort as the antichrist. The antichrist has been variously identified as Stalin, Hitler, the Pope, Saddam Hussein, the World Bank, Bill Gates and the World Council of Churches. What John in his epistles and the Bible more widely wants us to do is to identify and recognize the antichrists for what they are and stand firm against them.

▶ How has the antichrist been identified to you? Is it, as suggested above, a world leader or a political or social influence?

▶ Why are some people so concerned to deceive and undermine the faith of those who belong to Jesus Christ?

One of the characteristics of the end times is that there will be those around who will seek to deceive and undermine the faith of those who belong to Jesus Christ. John in his epistle is the only Biblical writer who actually uses the term antichrist, but the theme is seen elsewhere:

▶ Matthew 24 and Mark 13 refer to false Christs who will lead people astray, even those who belong to Christ.

▶ 2 Thessalonians 2 refers to the man of lawlessness, who opposes God and the spiritual realms as well as all other powers, and exalts himself.

▶ Revelation 12 and 13 mention the beast who blasphemes and seeks to deceive those who are perishing.

▶ 1 John 2 and 2 John refer to those who deny Jesus as the Christ.

A powerful antichrist figure is a key part of Christian teaching, both that of Jesus and that of the writers of the epistles. Who this antichrist figure is has not been specified. It might be a person or organization, or it might be a force of evil deliberately seeking to pervade people's minds. It could be a whole movement.

Antichrist means two things: firstly it is one who opposes God who comes openly and clearly as an adversary of the truth and of God himself, and secondly, it is those who come as imitators of Christ, who have a pretence of godliness, an appearance of holiness, but whose motivation is to destroy the truth.

At the final end of time a powerful antichrist will arise, but he will be preceded by lesser antichrist figures. The purpose of these characters is to deceive and take people away from the truth. Mostly in Biblical teaching these antichrists attack the people of God from without, but in

1 John 2 and 2 John the focus is very much on attacks on the people of God from within.

In the epistles of John, antichrists appear as imitation Christians, as an advance preview of the final antichrist figure. They are wolves in sheep's clothing, as Jesus warned his disciples (Matthew 7:15). They subtly seek to take the place of Christ, to undermine the faith and foundation of the Christian community. Just as Christ is the incarnation of God, so here the false teachers as the antichrists are the incarnation of evil.

They can look proper and well mannered, there is a superficial charm about them, but John unmasks these people for what they really are. They are false and evil teachers inspired by false and evil spirits, and their battleground is the minds and hearts of believers.

What began as a theological dispute over the person of Jesus Christ ended in immoral and divisive behaviour. The community, instead of being bonded together in love, was being torn apart by hatred. John uses strong language to condemn them as liars (2:22). In fact they have spoken the lie of all lies. To deny Jesus is the Christ is the source of all other lies. They cannot know the Father if they don't know the Son. They cannot know God's character and activity if they don't know the saving power of Jesus Christ. There is no compromise – the bottom line, the benchmark, the litmus test of faith, the final evidence when all is said and done, is the confession that Jesus is Lord, Jesus is the Christ; everything else comes from that (2:23; cf. 1 Corinthians 12:3).

The antichrists today

Who are the people who deny Jesus is Lord, who come with wonderful ideas, plans and schemes that sound good but do not come from Christ? Just because something is good doesn't mean it is right. There are so many antichrists around, whispering in our ears, dazzling our eyes and winning our hearts. Relativism is perhaps the biggest threat to us as God's people: the idea that there are no absolutes, that there is no right or wrong, those who say it might be right for you but something else is right for me, who argue that there is no objective truth, that truth is in the mind of the believer just as beauty is in the eye of the beholder.

So we are not allowed to comment negatively on someone's lifestyle, their sexual orientation, their relationships, their belief system. We hesitate to say 'Jesus is the only way to God', we are embarrassed about saying Jesus is 'the Way, the Truth and the Life'. Truth in a relativistic world is almost a four-letter word.

Some churches have packaged 'the truth' to make it palatable to a world of relativism. They know that people only like to think about nice things, positive and encouraging ideas, so the cross is no longer preached, and suffering, pain and sacrifice are ignored. The softer issues of God's grace and kindness, God's love and forgiveness, God as the eternal therapist, are emphasized.

Other churches in a spirit of ecumenism or liberal thought reinterpret the lordship of Christ so that it becomes a global force of moral good without any spiritual truth or absolutes as its basis. It is happening all around us. The gospel has been neutered for many people. People call themselves Christians and yet do not believe in a life-transforming message of salvation. Many churches are in decline numerically because they have nothing to offer a dying world. They have been seduced by attractive-looking ideas that deny the truth and power of the gospel.

The Bishop of Bologna said the following in one of his public addresses: 'The antichrist is not going to look like a beast but is much more likely to come as a philanthropist. He will appear charitable and kind, but this will mask his real aim – the destruction of Christianity and the "death of God". The antichrist will be politically correct, will take up all the good causes of pacifism, vegetarianism, environmentalism and animal rights. He will promote vague and fashionable values, humanitarian aid and ecology, and the feel-good factor will replace trust in Christ' (*The Times*, May 2000).

▶ What do you consider to be the most dangerous influences in your society that are seeking to undermine the kingdom of God? Would you agree with the Bishop of Bologna that the most damaging influences are fashionable and vague notions of spirituality and truth?

▶ Describe occasions when you or those whom you have known have been deceived and have abandoned or been tempted to abandon faith in Jesus Christ. What was the effect on the person and on the community of faith?

1 John 2:24–29

Continue in the confidence of God's anointing

John appeals to his readers to be persistent in their commitment to the truth and to allow the Holy Spirit to lead them as they move forward in their faith.

In this section of his letter John makes a simple appeal to his readers that they should remain loyal to all that they have known of Christ. So many people have wandered from the truth or have been tempted at some point to drift from their faith in Christ. John is no idealist; he understands the human heart and the distractions and digressions that can occur in life. He urges his readers not to depart from their original knowledge and grasp of the truth. John reminds them that it is worth remaining steadfast to the message they have known to be the truth. He implores them to remain in the truth – the truth that they originally heard, that they believed, and by which they were transformed. This will lead to all the promises of Jesus being fulfilled in them: promises of life, eternal life, life in the richest, fullest dimensions.

Throughout these verses there is a profound sense of John's concern for the people he writes to. He is anxious that they should stand firm and not be side-tracked by others, but he is a wise counsellor. He does not seek to control them. He knows that they have the ability to stand alone in the power of the Holy Spirit. His words encourage them to be confident in the grace God has given them and to trust the understanding they have already received. Good advice to anyone – hold on to the anointing you have received, and seek God for yourself when you are uncertain about an issue. The Holy Spirit is the one who will lead us into all truth (John 16:13).

It is not that those to whom John writes don't need his teaching, as clearly they do, but as they receive teaching from the Apostle and discuss together the Holy Spirit will guide and lead them and keep them in the truth.

There will always be people who come with new and seemingly more exciting ideas that tickle our ears (2 Timothy 4:3), and there will always be those who seek teaching to support their personal preferences in life. John's message is to avoid such people and hold on to the basis of your faith, the life you received when the gospel message was first revealed to you. We are encouraged to hold on to Christ and remain closely linked to him and not to all the new and novel ideas that are around.

In this brief section of the letter, three times John emphasizes the need to persist in the faith they have: 'See that what you have heard ... remains in you' (verse 24), 'remain in him' (verse 27), 'continue in him' (verse 28). John's expectation was that Jesus would return within their lifetime and he was concerned that his readers would not be embarrassed when they meet with their Lord. John has in mind here the themes he has previously addressed, of being loyal to the truth of Christ and living in a way that reflects the truth of Christ's teaching. As a pastor with integrity he is concerned to present his flock mature in

Christ, 'rooted and built up in him' (Colossians 2:7). It is no good starting the journey of faith if you can't keep going.

At first reading verse 29 is tricky to understand and might be taken by some to mean that anyone who is good and lives a virtuous life is a child of God. However, that would be a misunderstanding of John's teaching. Righteousness is a word with spiritual as well as moral implications. When John speaks of everyone doing what is right he is referring to more than just an exemplary lifestyle from an ethical perspective. Doing what is right involves worship, includes beliefs and has at its foundation a commitment to Jesus Christ as Lord. In speaking of those who are God's children, the rest of John's writing shows clearly that it is not those who are pleasant or seemingly virtuous but those who honour Jesus in all they do. Jesus' own teaching (Matthew 5:6, 10–11) shows that being right before God is much more than just being judged a 'good' person by the contemporary culture.

Questions

1. Why does counterfeit teaching sometimes appear so attractive and appealing within the church community?
2. John asks us to persist in our faith by remaining in the Son (verses 24 and 27) and continuing in him (verse 28). How can we do this in practice? Consider Hebrews 12:2–3.
3. Do you think that the church worldwide has remained devoted to the truth it has heard from the beginning? Can you think of examples of when it has failed to do so?

Jesus – fully human and fully divine

From the earliest days of the church there has been discussion about the person of Jesus Christ. Partly this was because of the Greek culture in which the church developed, with its view of the flesh as evil and unworthy of any deity. Partly, also, the discussion arose because of the difficulty of comprehending God as both fully human and fully divine.

Biblical Christian teaching is that Jesus was fully divine and fully human from his birth, throughout his lifetime and at his death. In order to be truly human he needed to empty himself of many of the divine prerogatives (Philippians 2:7–8), without taking on the sinful nature of humanity.

Only by being human and divine could Jesus be an effective sacrifice and a successful mediator of a new covenant. If Jesus had not been divine he would not have been the vehicle of God's grace, nor would he be without sin. Only a sinless sacrifice was adequate as the offering for the sin of the whole of humanity. If he had not been human he would not have been able to fully identify with the frailty of humanity or have been able to make an offering of his life.

It was necessary for God to become man that he might make atonement for sin. Romans 5:18–19 explains that, just as sin came into the world through one person – Adam, so righteousness comes through one person – Jesus Christ. It was the disobedience of Adam that brought death, and the obedience of Jesus Christ that brought life.

Jesus needed to be human in order to offer the gift of resurrection to all those who believe (1 Corinthians 15:45–49). He is the first fruits of the resurrection, opening the way for others to follow him. As a human being Jesus is able to help others in their needs (Hebrews 4:15 – 5:2) and he is also the perfect example to others of how to live as obedient servants of God (Philippians 2:5–8).

The heresy most likely to be at the forefront of John's mind as he wrote his letters was Docetism. This was a frequent threat to Christian orthodoxy as it claimed that Jesus was God clothed in a body that had the impression of humanity but wasn't really fully human. Some forms of Docetism suggested that the divine Logos adopted the person of Jesus at his baptism and left him before his crucifixion, since they believed God could neither be born nor die in human flesh. This denies the whole doctrine of atonement, of the need for a perfect human being to offer their lives willingly as a sacrifice.

The second coming

A key Christian belief is that Jesus Christ will return to earth at the end of history. At his second coming he will be seen by all and his glory will be recognized, unlike when he first walked the earth.

Many amongst the believers who knew Jesus as he lived on earth and the first generation of Christians expected Jesus to return in their lifetime. This expectation was largely based on Jesus' own teaching about the imminence of the kingdom of God (Matthew 24:30–34). However, teaching on the imminence of the kingdom of God has much more to do with the fact that the kingdom of God is never far away, always ready to break in when a person responds to the gospel message, than the consummation of history and the end of time.

The second coming is the time when the dead are raised, the world is judged, and all evil and opposition to God is destroyed. It will be the fulfilment of all God's plans for his kingdom and his people. Christians are encouraged to be patient, to be prepared for his return, and to watch for signs that his kingdom is coming.

The second coming is foretold in the Old Testament (Daniel 7:13–14) and by Jesus himself (Mark 13:26). The Bible teaches that before the second coming occurs a number of events will take place:

▶ The gospel will be preached to the whole world (Matthew 24:14)

▶ Christians will be persecuted (Luke 21:12)

▶ Godlessness will abound (2 Peter 3:3–4)

▶ The antichrist will be revealed (1 John 2:18)

▶ There will be false prophets and false Christs (Mark 13:22)

▶ There will be wars, famines and earthquakes (Matthew 24:6–8)

The second coming will occur at God's appointed time, but it will be unexpected (1 Thessalonians 5:1–2). It will happen after a delay (Matthew 25:5) but, paradoxically, it is also imminent (James 5:8–9).

The purpose of the second coming will be to restore and renew all things (Revelation 21:1–5). As part of this process the dead will be raised (1 Corinthians 15:22–23) and all will be judged (Romans 2:5). All evil and opposition to God will be destroyed (2 Thessalonians 2:8) and Jesus Christ will bring final salvation to all those who are waiting for him (Hebrews 9:28).

1 John 3:1–6

God's extravagant love

A celebration of God's love and generosity. A reminder that it is Christ who deals with the problem of sin and makes it possible for us to know this love.

John has just written to his readers about their need to continue in Christ and remain in the family relationship, which God has so generously made available to them. John then launches into these marvellous words that remind us of the greatness of God's love. The notion

(2:29) that all those who know him are born of him, making them his children, prompts John's words about the astonishing love and kindness of God. It would be good for us to pause for a moment at verse 1 and reflect on how awesome the thoughts are in this single verse.

This love from the Father is a love that sees us in our weakness and our selfishness. It is not a blind love that ignores all our wrongdoing and pride, our rebellion and unholiness. It is a love that knows the whole truth about us and still loves us so much that we are made members of the family. We are given the status of sons and daughters of God, with an inheritance deserved only by the perfect. We don't have a God who seeks to catch us out, or trip us up or exclude us from all that is good. We have a God whose love is so immense, his bigheartedness so wide, that even knowing us at our worst he accepts us as his own, receives us into his family and blesses us with all the riches that are his to give. These riches include a future inheritance in glory, a peace for the present, the truth of salvation, his love, and the work of his Holy Spirit amongst us.

The language used in this verse is the language of superlatives, of being unmeasured and overwhelming. God's love is seen as extravagant, profligate, deluging and engulfing. The love that God has for us is not only shown when we are obedient and following his plans; it is lavished upon us at all times – we are smothered with his love. His love is there supporting, leading, comforting, guiding and embracing those who are in Christ.

In the year 2000 in many parts of England, there were destructive floods that engulfed a number of towns and cities. The effect was horrendous. The flood water flowed with such force that it engulfed everything in its way. God's love can be likened to a flood tide that sweeps into believers' lives; it transforms and restores. The recipient is helpless to resist when God's love is revealed in such power and strength.

I was speaking recently with a young woman named Paula, who is half-way through an Alpha course and is just discovering the overwhelming love of God. Every night before bed she takes her Bible into the bath with her and reads. With three children it is her only opportunity for peace. Every night she is reduced to tears. She is moved and challenged that God loves her so completely, that God is at work in her life, that the love of God can change her and move her forward.

God is incredible in the love that he shows. He is more than generous, giving believers a status and standing that is barely conceivable. Those who believe in Jesus Christ are children of God. The King of Kings calls us children – not servants, not slaves – but part of the family. By nature we are creatures, created by the Lord of the universe. We are born as God's created beings but by God's grace we are family. God is our Father, a unique bond: a close, intimate relationship of acceptance and affection.

Christians have this astonishing relationship and yet it goes unrecognized by the majority of those around us. Those who do not have a relationship with God through Christ cannot recognize those who are his children. It's as if we were in a foreign country and seeing all the different uniforms. We might not recognize the police, the army, the paramedics and other officials. So it is with God's people; those who do not know the Father cannot identify the Father's children. People outside of the Christian family do not recognize the church for what it truly is because they do not understand the significance of the activities of God and his people.

John continues in his thinking (verse 2); his mind leads him to reflect that if they are already children of God with all the blessings that entails, what else might be in store? He doesn't know clearly what the future will be like when Christ returns (Matthew 25:31) and we are changed and are with him, but if what they are already experiencing is so good then the future must be fantastic.

I have heard on a number of occasions Christians express some concern about their future in eternity. It is so difficult for us to grasp what we will be like and what our existence in the new heaven and the new earth will be.

Some have even gone so far as to suggest if their husband or wife, son or daughter or even favourite pet isn't there, then they don't want to go. That is to misunderstand eternity completely. We cannot grasp the truth of the future in eternity with God because our minds cannot take it in; we still have our unspiritual nature that prevents us grasping all the truth about our future in glory. What we do know is that when we come into our full inheritance with Christ then we will be in a perfect relationship with God: we will know the love of God fully. Nothing else will matter. This love will be so great and so overwhelming that we will be fully content, totally satisfied and without any dissatisfaction.

When Christ is fully revealed at his second coming it will have a transforming effect on his followers: 'we shall be like him, for we shall see him as he is' (verse 2). Those who know him as Lord and Christ will become like him in their resurrection bodies. What exactly this will mean is incomprehensible to us at this finite time of our lives, but one day we will leave behind the problems and routines of this life and have a focus that is fully Christ-centred.

Knowing that Christ will return and that we will be like him has a tangible effect in people's lives. This hope is not just wishful thinking: it is a transforming influence. The honour and spotlessness of Christ does not leave us unaltered even as we think about him. His character and example makes his people ever more pure and righteous.

John returns to the theme of sin and its seriousness in the lives of all people, believers or unbelievers. I earlier likened the letter of John to the London Eye, a huge Ferris wheel on the south bank of the River Thames in the centre of London. As the pod travels up and around the huge Ferris wheel, familiar scenes are viewed from different points and therefore fresh insight is gained into the sites. These verses take us back to the theme of sin, already looked at in 1 John 1:8 – 2:2 and to be visited again in the final chapter of this letter. Sin is viewed from a different angle and fresh insight is gained from the new vantage point.

John defines sin as breaking the law, not the civil or criminal law that we may be familiar with, but the law of God, which is much broader and inclusive in its boundaries. Under the laws of most nations a person would not be guilty of breaking the law by having wrong attitudes, such as greed. They are only guilty of breaking the law of the land if they *act* in an illegal way. So a person breaks the law if they murder someone, but does not break the law if they hate someone.

The law of God, which John refers to, is the law that covers the whole plan of God for the way we live: the way we relate to people, the way we work, how we spend our leisure time, our use of our money, and a whole range of other issues of life. Jesus summed up the whole of the Law and the Prophets with these words, 'Love the Lord your God with all your heart and with all your soul and with all your mind' and 'Love your neighbour as yourself' (Matthew 22:37, 39). In this way we can understand how those who sin, who do not keep God's perfect standards of love, break the law. Any sin, by definition, is failing to live up to God's standards of perfection, and therefore sin is also lawlessness.

This dismal picture of us all being lawbreakers, seemingly without hope, is immediately counterbalanced with a reminder of Christ, the solution to the problem of sin. We may all be lawbreakers and therefore under the law, deserving punishment, but Christ, who is without sin, who never broke God's law in word, action or thought, is able to deal with the problem of sin, the problem of our failure to live up to God's ideal of love. His death was the punishment for our sin, and his resurrection was the victory over sin so that sin no longer has a hold on those who believe in Christ.

Verse 6 does not mean that as Christians we become sinless and no longer sin. Down the centuries there has been a tradition within the church which has claimed just that. Some within the Holiness Movement claim that by the power of the Holy Spirit Christians can be fully sanctified, in this life on earth, and be free from sin. That is a misunderstanding of Biblical teaching and does not take note of a number of passages that refer to our 'old sinful nature' (for example, Romans 7:14–25) that remains until we are fully transformed by Christ when he returns.

The suggestion that Christians can be or are sinless would also contradict what John has already said in 1 John 1:8: 'If we claim to be without sin, we deceive ourselves and the truth is not in us.' The meaning therefore of verse 6 is that when we become Christians sin no longer has us captive, and we no longer have the intention to sin. There is still the old nature that leads us to behave in ungodly ways, but the intention and desire of the believer is not to break God's law. Those who do not know Christ have no intention to resist sin, and may even enjoy their failure to keep God's standards. Those who wallow in activities that are contrary to God's kingdom and have no inclination to decline sin's temptation cannot have known the transforming power of God at work in their lives through Christ.

Let me illustrate this from an everyday example of greed and materialism. Many of us would like an improved material lifestyle – a newer car, a bigger house, exotic holidays. Believers and unbelievers fail to live up to God's ideal by being discontented and envious and always wanting something more. The Christian will fail in this area of life but their intention will be to resist the temptation and seek to be Christ-centred in their material possessions. The Christian will want to do what is right as far as material possessions are concerned. The unbeliever will have no intention of resisting this temptation to break God's ideal. They will do all they can, with little hesitation, to improve their lifestyle materially and have little intention of being content with what they have.

Questions

1. What are the privileges and what are the responsibilities of being loved so extravagantly by God?

2. Has the church been in danger of emphasizing the extravagant love of God and yet not taking seriously enough the significance of sin? Is it possible that an emphasis on love makes the church become 'soft' with sin? How can we achieve the right emphasis on both?
3. Meditate on God's love. Read 1 John 3:1 several times in three different versions. Read aloud Ephesians 3:16–19. Ask God to give you a fresh awareness of his extravagant love. After a few moments of waiting on God, thank him and worship him for his love.

1 John 3:7–10

Children of the devil exposed

John is aware of just how easy it is for Christians to be tempted away from faith. He suggests a way of discerning those who have destructive motives.

John reinforces his deep concern for his readers, referring to them affectionately as 'dear children' and being anxious for them that they remain in the truth and not be led away from it. It is so easy, he realizes, for those with mischievous intent to distract believers from the transforming truth of Christ's work. John gives his readers a way of distinguishing between those with a focus on Christ and his gospel and those who are mischievously seeking other ends. As we have already explained, there were those at the time this letter was being written who were claiming the truth, and yet in fact what they were teaching was not the gospel of Christ but their own ideas and thoughts encouraged by the devil. They were leading others astray, taking them from the truth of the gospel and leading them to a spiritual land of wilderness and desert.

We need to be aware today of those who would lead us astray and take us from the truth of the gospel. It is easy to think we are too wise or understanding or informed to be led astray, and yet it can and does happen with sad regularity. Perhaps the most obvious way in which believers today might be led astray is by those belonging to cults. There are many around who focus on Christians as a soft target for the ideas they are peddling. There are many heartbreaking stories of those who have been beguiled by apparently attractive arguments that have led them away from their families and faith in Christ. The Children of God, founded by David Berg in the 1970s, which encouraged promiscuity amongst his followers, and the Solar Temple Cult, whose adherents were either murdered or committed suicide between 1994 and 1997 in France, Switzerland and Canada, are two examples of cults that taught corrupt and disturbing spiritual material.

But deception can be very subtle. Any idea or belief, philosophy or approach to life that does not have Christ at the centre is likely to deceive. One of the trends in business in recent years has been to include an ethos and belief system in the company policy: ethics and strategies that all staff are expected to adhere to and be committed to. Such business belief systems can be misleading and harmful in the way that they package marketing strategy as seeming truth, when in fact it might deny some of the basic Christian truths of the gospel. Christian business personnel might be so caught up in the framework of a company's mission statement, ethos and policy that they lose sight of Christ at the centre their lives.

I think also of how in recent years in education the emphasis has been on excellence, raising standards and improving results. It is so easy to be carried away by such persuasive talk and yet fail to connect our thinking with the gospel of Christ. In the area where I live the emphasis for children is on achievement. It seems that children today have to succeed in music, sport, maths, literacy, information technology and science by the time they are ten years old. Even Christian people have been led astray by thinking that what really matters is a good education and high attainment, whereas the gospel of Christ tells us that what really matters is a relationship with God, an acknowledgement that Jesus is Lord. It may be that what leads us astray is much more subtle than it used to be, or maybe we have so many distractions that our focus on Christ is so easily lost. Whatever the reasons, the danger of being led astray is as great today as it was in the first century, if not more so. Even good things like education can be sinful when they are made into an end in themselves.

In order to distinguish those who have the potential to lead astray, John links actions and beliefs. This is a link many of the New Testament writers have made, particularly James: 'What good is it, my brothers, if a man claims to have faith but has no deeds?' (James 2:14). It is those who live with integrity in the gospel who are the people of the truth, just as Jesus the Messiah lived with integrity and showed he is the truth of God. For believers there should be no discrepancy between what is believed and behaviour. One should lead to the other. As Christ is the truth of God incarnate, so he lived a life of truth. The litmus test of true faith is therefore the actions of the individual. The person who belongs to Christ will be righteous and will be seeking to live righteously.

Those who do not have Christ as Lord live in a state of separation from God and they are led into wrong actions. Their unwillingness to acknowledge Jesus as the Christ is evidence enough that they are part of the devil's scheme to undermine the kingdom of God. Those who habitually sin, who consistently refuse to trust God, who reject God's ideal and plan and who have little consideration for truth are following the leading of the evil one and participating in his plans of maintaining humanity's separation from God.

There is a danger we expect those who are 'of the devil' to somehow be seen to be evil and wicked and obviously devilish in all they do. The problem of course is that sin may be socially acceptable. Those who are of the devil are likely to be our thoroughly pleasant and kind neighbours who share our lives, our joys and our sorrows. They don't get in trouble with the police, they are model citizens, and put to shame some of us Christians they live alongside. The issue is what is their focus of life. Without Christ, the focus is inevitably self or some other idol. They may be the best neighbours but their motivation and world view will be alien to the gospel focus and Christ's lordship.

It seems a harsh judgment to call these people 'of the devil', yet the words of Jesus himself remind us that 'He who is not with me is against me, and he who does not gather with me scatters (Matthew 12:30). A pound coin which is currency in the UK cannot be used in the USA. It is only coins with the authority of the USA government on them that can be used in the USA. Similarly, there are those who are 'of the devil' because that is who they owe their allegiance to and not Jesus Christ, even though on the surface and in many other ways they appear similar to those who do belong to Jesus Christ.

That is the bad news, but the good news is that Jesus has come to destroy the devil's work, to ensure that there is a restoration of the relationship between God and humanity. The whole world, its structures, politics and power struggles are in the grip of Satan. At the fall, when sin entered the world, the devil gained dominance over all human authorities and powers. Christ has come to defeat Satan and to win back the world for God, which he did when he died on the cross, so that those in Christ are no longer surrendered to the powers of darkness but have the freedom of a relationship with God.

The logic of John's argument continues in verse 9. Those who are born of the Spirit, who receive new life through Christ, will not continue to sin because they have the seed of God's presence in them. God cannot cohabit with sin. Christians will be dissatisfied with the sin in their lives and be constantly confessing and seeking forgiveness for any wrongdoing, and allowing God's grace to transform them into what he wants his people to be.

John concludes his thoughts on sin with the litmus test of faith. The children of God are distinguished from the children of the devil by their actions and lifestyle. Those who do what is right, remembering that doing what is right includes the whole span of God's truth (2:9), are children of God. Those who do not do what is right are children of the devil. Doing what is right particularly includes loving their brothers and sisters in Christ.

I wonder how many people would be excluded from our churches if we imposed this test on them. If we had some way of measuring whether they love others, would we be pleasantly surprised or horrified by the results? It is a salutary reminder that so many of the disagreements that arise in church come from the devil. The absence of love in discussions and debates is not God's way of moving forward. To show love is to respect and honour others as well as care for them. It is patently obvious that we fail to do this in many of our church disputes across the whole spectrum of Christian organizations and denominations. We must confess our tardiness in showing love and be prepared to seek God's grace to love the unlikeable.

Questions

1. Suggest and discuss ways in which the devil is presenting sin as acceptable. How do we discern when an influence is destructive and harmful and should therefore be resisted?
2. Good basic relationships in churches seem so rare. Why is this so, and how can love be put at the heart of our Christian communities?
3. Are some sins worse than others? How would you prioritize sin in terms of its seriousness before God and in a Christian community?

The world

'The world' conjures up all manner of images and pictures for us. Travels to far away places, or being a person of experience and savvy as in 'man of the world'. In the Bible, too, the term has a number of different meanings. God created the world and declared it to be good (Genesis 1:31). After the fall, sin entered the world, contaminating it and making it a threat to believers (Romans 5:12–14). Christians have to live in the world, but need to remain distinct from the world and recognize that the world can be a temptation and enticement away from God's kingdom (1 John 2:16).

At the fall when Adam and Eve disobeyed God and allowed sin into the world, all of creation was affected and all of creation came under the power of Satan, as 1 John 4:4 indicates. The world is under the control of the evil one (1 John 5:19) and is in rebellion against God. Pride, sensual desire and immorality are some of the evidence that the world has rebelled against God and is opposed to all that the kingdom of heaven stands for (1 John 2:15–17).

It only takes a glimpse at a newspaper to recognize how far the world has strayed from the perfect creation that God intended. Greed, immorality, violence, pride and selfishness dominate the news. These are the characteristics of a world under the control of the evil one. This is the context in which Christians live their daily lives, and from which they have been saved. Believers are called to resist the attractions of the world that appeal to their old nature, and to be distinctive and pure, set apart for God, by living a life that is holy and blameless.

The evil power and control of Satan in this world extends to unseen and heavenly realms. Ephesians 6:12 reminds believers that the spiritual battles are not what they might seem on the surface, but are against the powers and rulers of this dark world. The evidence of evil forces in the spiritual realms is seen in the destructive nature of communities in the physical world.

A number of Bible passages indicate that the world, under the control of the evil one, is only a passing phase. The world is under judgment and will be condemned; it will not last for ever (1 John 2:17). The world will be judged (Acts 17:31), it will be judged justly, but will be found to be guilty by God's righteousness.

LIVE IN LOVE, REJECT WHAT IS FALSE

1 John 3:11 – 5:21

Stop and look

The first 'Stop and look' in part 1 talked about the author-ship and background to this letter. At the start of the second study in John's letters, here are a few guidelines about what you should look out for and the issues that will be covered. John continues to be concerned for the faith and stability of the Christian communities to whom he is writing. He wants their faith and belief to be seen in their behaviour, and for them to recognize that true faith leads to godly living and flawed teaching leads to ungodly living.

The main themes in this section are:

▶ The overwhelming love of God seen in Christ

▶ The confidence that is the believers' inheritance when they come to faith

▶ The need to be discerning and recognize falsehood

▶ The importance of holy living and keeping free from sin

1 John 3:11–18

Love: not like Cain, like Jesus

Love is at the heart of Christian faith. All of those who are believers in Jesus Christ should follow his example of selfless love and not follow the example of Cain, who was embittered by his own self-centredness.

We come to a central point of John's letter, to an issue he is concerned that his readers grasp more than any other. He wants them to understand that at the heart of Christian faith is not a formal set of doctrines or beliefs, not a barren orthodoxy or theological correctness, but a life-changing, life-enhancing, community-transforming love. When they first discovered that God was there for them, it was his gracious and astounding love that wooed and won them. The believers need to love each other as God has loved them because, apart from any other reason, they need the support and help of each other. This is particularly the case in the context of the bad relationships and discord they were experiencing from those outside of the family of God who were causing upset and stirring up trouble amongst them, leading to division and the breaking down of relationships.

John reflects that this is not a new situation. From the earliest days of the Old Testament, in the story of Cain and Abel, resentment against those God chose to bless has been apparent. Cain was consumed with jealousy because of the favour his brother Abel found with God, and so he murdered him (Genesis 4:2–8). The people of God, those who are Christians and trust in Jesus as the Christ, are at times hated by those around. The presence of God's people acts like a catalyst to those who are evil. The presence of the

Spirit of God is inflammatory to the evil one and brings about uncalled-for hatred and negative actions.

It is important to note that John's acid test of being a true follower of Christ, of having passed from death to life, is the test of love: not a cerebral knowledge or intellectual understanding, not even a clear grasp of all that the gospel means and intends. The acid test is, have we been filled with love? Has our experience of Christ made us more loving, has it filled us with a genuine generosity of spirit towards others? It is sad how frequently those who are concerned to check the authenticity of faith in others approach them with arrogance, insensitivity and little evidence of kindness and warmth.

I remember visiting a small fellowship in the United States when on holiday. We enjoyed the worship and appreciated being part of a rural community that loved the Lord. However, in our conversations at the end of the service it was apparent that a few people were suspicious of us as visitors from a long way away. There was little love shown: we were questioned on our beliefs and there was an unspoken accusation that we weren't really people true to the word of God. I got the distinct impression that city people were too sophisticated to hold to the simple gospel truth that meant so much to them. They may have had a point, but their absence of love and welcome was not evidence of the simple gospel truth that they claimed to hold to so strongly. Their manner to us was distrustful and their attitude cool and distant, not the love we are encouraged to share with one another in Christ.

God's people need to love each other, support and be committed to each other in the face of opposition from others, but it is that very love that promotes the hatred of those who are evil. We should not be surprised if some of the people in the local community we belong to find us insufferable. The qualities that the people of God should display – love, integrity, holiness and truth – tend to incite to anger and dislike those who live by a different set of values. The vitriolic attacks that Christians sometimes receive when they speak about ethical and spiritual issues is an indication of the hostility some feel towards the people of God.

The love that God has put in us is the evidence of having passed from death to life. It is this love that is our strength and our foundation, but also it is this love that causes such problems. God's love is a reminder to those outside of Christ that they have not received life, but are on the pathway to death. The absence of self-giving, sacrificial love is an indication of a person who is separated from God and remains spiritually dead, with no hope of eternal life.

It appears that verse 15 takes us into even tougher territory. 'Anyone who hates his brother is a murderer' may be a little hard for us to accept. It is John's way of emphasizing the importance of love. In our straightforward way of looking at life, it seems that it must be worse to murder someone than just to hate them. We must remember, however, that John is not writing about social issues and criminal justice, but about spiritual truth. In the world of policing and law courts, social order and community stability, then to murder is far worse than to hate. In the context of God's law, however, of the spiritual demands to love and serve each other, then to hate is to break God's law.

To hate means if we were given the opportunity we would murder. It arises from self-interest, from a determination that our will should be allowed full expression and that anyone who obstructs what we want should be removed. This hatred is prevalent in our world at the time of writing. In many countries where there is ethnic tension and strife, hatred readily leads to murder, as we know only too well from the destruction of the World Trade Centre. The willingness to accommodate hateful thoughts indicates a willingness to murder if the circumstances allow. Hatred is not just an irritation and frustration with someone because they are not likeable; it is an obsessive desire to eliminate someone because of a deep-seated antagonism to them.

To want to take the life of someone is evidence that a

person does not have eternal life. Murder is a particularly heinous crime because it cannot be reversed. All are made in the image of God, whether they know Christ or not, and murder extinguishes someone created with the stamp of God. To hate, to murder, to be in bad relationships with other people, is characteristic of a world leading to death. To love and support and be in harmonious relationships are the features of lives based on the truth and teaching of God.

Having stated the importance of love for the believer, this letter goes on to illustrate more fully what this love truly means. It is in Jesus Christ that love is seen at its most candid. In an echo of similar thoughts in John's Gospel, 'Greater love has no-one than this, that he lay down his life for his friends' (John 15:13), John speaks of Jesus giving up his life at his crucifixion and encourages the followers of Jesus to imitate his example. At first sight it seems as if John might be expecting all Christians to become martyrs and to be prepared to die for their faith and for each other. In some circumstances around the world today that is the reality that faces those who love Christ. In Pakistan, Thailand, Burundi, Rwanda and many other nations in recent years, there have been those who have given up their lives in love for their Lord.

However, John explains the meaning of what he is saying in more tangible ways for those of us who do not face such drastic possibilities. To love means to care for others, to support them and, if it is in our power to do so, to provide for those in need. He gives the practical example of someone having plenty and being prepared to share it with others who are without.

The definitive example of love is found in Christ himself, he who did not seek to have his own way or promote his own rights or power. True love as revealed in Christ is sacrificial, willing to suffer for others, prepared to give up creature comforts and worldly status, to be humble and considerate. Just as Christ has laid down his life for others, so we should lay down our lives in love for those around us. This is a huge and demanding requirement, and is yet another reminder that being a Christian is not just a matter of what we believe and think, our attitudes and our values; it is a matter of action, of using all that God has so generously given us to love and reach others.

It is so easy to be full of all the latest spiritual language, to talk endlessly about love in a sentimental or theoretical manner, without ever showing that love in action. It so often happens that the needier members of our fellowships are overlooked, those on the margins who perhaps aren't the most entertaining or the easiest to befriend or welcome into our homes. If we are loving as Christ requires then we should recognize those in need of love and reach out to them as God has reached out to us. It is all too easy to share God's love and care only with those who are like us, those who have similar lifestyles and interests and talk about the same things. The way of Christ is to share God's love with those in need in God's family. That is how we know we belong to the truth, and how we know God is at work in our lives.

Questions

1. Have Christian communities been compromising in order to avoid the hatred of the surrounding society?
2. Why is loving our brothers and sisters in Christ sometimes so difficult? Share ways in which God is calling you to be more loving in your current circumstances.
3. Discuss why, in God's view, to hate is to be like a murderer. Suggest reasons why treating all sin equally would be a poor basis for state law.
4. What do you think are the implications of verse 17 for relationships between churches internationally? Put in the words 'African' or 'Asian' or 'South American' before 'brother'. What effect does this have?

Stop and think: Love

To write about love in just a few words can never do justice to a theme that is the essence of God and the basic command to Christians. Jesus said, '"Love the Lord your God with all your heart and with all your soul and with all your mind." This is the first and greatest commandment. And the second is like it: "Love your neighbour as yourself"' (Matthew 22:37–39). To love God and to love others is the epitome of Christian discipleship.

▶ List the qualities you would expect to see in someone who is seeking to show the love of Christ. Use 1 Corinthians 13 to help you draw up this list.

▶ Is the love that is spoken of here only relevant to personal relationships or could it be a feature of national and social relationships?

In the context of 1 John the emphasis on love is particularly significant because of the false teachers and the danger to the community of believers of becoming defensive and suspicious of others in their attempts to keep their faith pure. When the true teaching of the gospel is being tested, as it was amongst the communities that John wrote to, it is easy to become guarded and mistrustful of those who might see things differently or who may be facing failure. When we feel threatened we don't love as we should, but retreat into self-protectionism.

Love has a greater concern for others than for self, which is why when we are tempted to be defensive we need to love all the more. It is easy to fall into the trap of replacing love with spirituality, to cling to gifts and ability when it is love that is needed. Too easily we speak of love when our failure to actually love is seen in a critical and judgmental spirit.

Jesus' example in washing the disciples' feet (John 13:1–15) and his use of the parable of the Good Samaritan (Luke 10:25–37) show the type of love that God wants his disciples to demonstrate to others. God wants a love that serves others and humbles itself, a love that cares for those who are different or not our type. Love is shown in deeds, although it begins with an attitude of the heart, a desire to honour God and do his will.

The greatest example of love is in Jesus offering his life for the sake of others. 'Greater love has no-one than this, that he lay down his life for his friends' (John 15:13). This is the ultimate requirement of love: to live sacrificially for others, even giving up our lives if required.

It can be a daily battle to show love. When someone we love is difficult or disappoints us or we are required to show selfless love day in and day out, then it is possible for our love to grow weary and fail. The love of Christ needs to be renewed within us daily so that we can be a constant source of love for others. We cannot love in our own strength; we must pray for the power of the Holy Spirit to give us the love we need each day for those around us. Our love leaks out as we get bumped and knocked in the routines of life. We need to be refilled regularly to ensure that when we do get knocked and bumped that what does come out is love.

There is a supernatural economy about love. All other resources in the world are depleted when they are shared. If I share my money I have less money for myself and less money to give to others tomorrow. If I use my time for one needy cause I do not have the time to be of use elsewhere. Love, however, has a multiplier effect. The more we share it, the more it grows. Our stocks of love are not depleted or reduced, but as love is shown so it increases and strengthens. We can afford to be generous with the love that God has given us. The more generous we are with God's love, the more it expands and spreads out to others.

▶ Is love a feeling, an action, a commitment or response to a person or situation?

▶ Suggest three practical ways in which you could allow the love of God to flow more readily through you. How might situations be transformed if God's love was sought more frequently by his followers?

1 John 3:19–24

Confidence and assurance before God

Having confidence before God is a matter of trust and obedience.

John's words about our hearts condemning us and having hearts at rest might have been written for the twenty-first century Christian. I meet with many Christian people who are full of insecurity and anxieties, believing they are not good enough for God and unable to accept themselves as loved by God. Many are tortured by doubts not about God but about themselves. 'Surely God can't use me or accept me', they say. We are often conscious of our inadequacies, but we need to hold on to the truth in verse 20 that God is much greater than our hearts. Our hearts condemn us; we fail and so self-condemnation is inevitable. But God is greater than our hearts; he knows our sin, our love, our longings, the hopes that are never fulfilled, our apologies. He knows all this and he accepts us. It is we who have trouble accepting ourselves. The perfect knowledge that God has of us is not our terror, but our hope. There are no secrets between us and God, and that should be a source of great comfort. God knows everything and loves us; he knows everything and wants us to be his children, part of the family. God knows everything and wants to change us from within to be like him.

These verses are a summary of all that John has already said as he reinforces the points that he wants his readers to understand. First in this section of the letter he speaks of the confidence that the believers should have before God. Their hearts should not condemn them and their approach to God can be without anxiety. This is not intended to encourage arrogance or self-righteousness; the confidence that Christians have is not self-confidence, but an assurance that God through Christ has made it possible for him to be approached. As it says in Hebrews 10:19, 'we have confidence to enter the Most Holy Place by the blood of Jesus'. It is the cross of Christ that enables us to go fearlessly into the presence of God. It is nothing of our own doing, but God's gracious love making it possible.

When a person returns from international travel to their own country, they have confidence to go through passport control because they are a citizen of that nation and they have the documents to prove it. Similarly, we can enter the presence of God because we are citizens of his kingdom. All that Christ did for us in dying and rising again is our proof and evidence of citizenship.

The next statement in John's letter could cause us some problems: 'and receive from him anything we ask' (verse 22). It sounds like a dream ticket to material prosperity, exotic holidays, mass healings, huge evangelistic success and a quick way to overcome all the difficulties of life. Simply ask God and we will receive.

Clearly this cannot mean what at first sight or in an immature way it might be taken to mean when it is removed from its context: 'Whatever I ask God for, he will give me because he is my loving Father.' I say clearly, because I know in my own life I have asked for things in prayer and not received them, and also because I know of great saints whom God has called to a ministry of prayer who have asked for things and have not received them. This has to be a deeper issue than a short cut to all the spiritual and material blessings we might desire.

When we interpret these words alongside other passages, such as later in this letter (1 John 5:14) and James 5:15 in the context of prayers for healing, there are insights that help us to learn what the teaching of this letter and of Scripture more widely is on prayer.

We should be glad that we do not receive everything we ask for in prayer, for some of us ask from very mixed motives (James 4:3). Many of us would be in dire straits if God had answered all our prayers and given us all we requested. I am grateful that prayers prayed with youthful enthusiasm but not much wisdom were answered by God with a clear 'No'. I can imagine all kinds of awful circumstances I would now be in if God had given me all that I wanted!

The teaching of this passage is not that God gives us everything we ask for, even when we ask for things that are outside of his will and purposes. This statement and other similar statements are about listening in prayer, hearing God's voice, knowing his will, and praying with confidence and authority because we are praying that God's will be done. So often we tag that little saying on to the end of our prayers, 'according to your will', thinking somehow that it makes the prayers acceptable. Maybe we should listen more to God in our prayers, seek his will more thoughtfully, and pray in the light of how we are led. So often our prayers are a list of needs and requests. Frequently our prayers could be summed up by the phrase 'Lord, make my life and their lives easier and more comfortable'. We don't mean to, but when we come up against a problem, whether it is suffering and illness, relationship problems, financial worries, lack of growth in the church or division in the fellowship, our request to God is in essence 'take the problem away'. Yet often God wants us to know him in that problem, to find his power at work through the problem, to be given boldness and confidence that even if the worst does happen then he is there to see us through.

Answered prayer is closely linked to obedience and doing what pleases God. When we are fully committed to the reign of Christ in our lives and seeking only to do what delights God, then we will be in harmony with the will of the heavenly Father in our prayers and he will respond and give us what we ask for. Many of us wish to short circuit the process and expect God to answer our prayers when they are far from his will and when we haven't submitted to him or acted in a way that honours him.

In the final verses of this chapter John explains more fully what obedience means for the believer. At its most fundamental level, obedience means to believe that Jesus is the Saviour, that he is the Son of God, and that God sent him to earth to do his will in dying and rising again. The second part of this obedience is loving each other. It is similar in essence to the words of Jesus to the teacher of the law who asked which is the greatest commandment. Jesus replied, '"Love the Lord your God with all your heart and with all your soul and with all your mind." This is the first and greatest commandment. And the second is like it: "Love your neighbour as yourself"' (Matthew 22:37–39). Both the words of Christ and the words of John sum up the whole Christian faith in these two commands: love God and love each other.

I wonder sometimes whether we make our faith far too complicated and get tied up with issues that lead us to forget the simple truth that God loves us and that Jesus died and rose again. There are times when all manner of church issues and personality clashes get in the way of us remembering the basic calling on our lives to love God and love each other.

The final verse of this chapter affirms the standing of those who are committed to Christ. Remember that the context of this letter is false teachers who had confused and undermined the faith of the believers, making the Christians doubt their salvation and bringing division amongst them. John reminds them that, contrary to what these false teachers have been saying, those who follow Christ live in Christ and Christ lives in them. The confirmation of this is the Spirit who is at work amongst them and through them. It is not difficult for influences to challenge our trust and faith in Christ, to make us wonder whether or not we truly are children of the King. If you doubt and need proof that God really is at work within you and Christ is the saviour of the world, then follow the pattern set here. Commit yourself to Christ, obey his teaching, seek his Holy Spirit to use you, and you will understand again the truth of the Christian message.

Questions

1. Discuss or reflect on occasions when you have been troubled by doubts or felt condemned before God. Explain how God has brought you through such times. What constructive things have you learnt from these experiences?
2. Do Christians today rely too heavily on their feelings to determine their spiritual strength? Or should we measure our spiritual life by obedience? How can obedience be measured?
3. The growth of postmodern perspectives has caused large numbers of people to doubt a faith based on absolutes. How can the church protect itself from the doubts and condemnation that come from contemporary influences that give no room for absolutes but are tolerant of everything?

Assurance

Lack of assurance of salvation and uncertainty about being accepted by God are frequent concerns for Christians, either for themselves or in supporting others. Those with low self-esteem or who lack confidence are the most vulnerable to an absence of assurance. However most, if not all, Christians struggle at times to be assured of God's love for them and the truth of what they believe. That is one of the reasons why John in his letters uses the word 'know' so frequently. He is concerned that the believers he is writing to should know the truth about Jesus Christ, and in knowing have confidence and assurance of the forgiveness of their sins and their relationship with God.

John knows that the false teachers have shaken the confidence of his readers. He therefore gives a number of reasons for assurance to encourage and strengthen them. The main basis for assurance is God's own witness through his Son (5:9–12). The life, teaching, death and resurrection of Jesus are all evidence that God is at work and that all who believe have eternal life.

A second basis for assurance is the witness of the Holy Spirit. It is the Holy Spirit (2:27) who gives believers confidence as they are led into truth. It is the Holy Spirit who is the proof or affirmation of God's grace in our lives (4:13). Too often we listen to voices around us rather than trust and hear the Holy Spirit who is within.

John also addresses the issue of assurance through prayer (3:21–22). We can be confident in prayer when we ask according to God's will. As we understand what it means to pray in God's will, to be obedient and sensitive to God's Spirit at work through prayer, then prayer becomes a means of gaining assurance of God's presence and power. We are reminded by 5:14 that when we pray with a clear conscience, because we have obeyed and pleased God, then answered prayer will increase our faith and our confidence in the truth of Jesus Christ.

A final theme that is linked to assurance is that of love. When we fulfil God's calling and command to be people of love, we gain assurance of our relationship with God. As we try to be people of love, and share the love we have received with others, then we cannot help but understand and gain confidence in God's love as he uses us as channels of unconditional love to others.

The grounds for assurance in the letters of John are not subjective but are based on objective evidence. It is first through belief in Jesus Christ as Saviour and Son of God, belief in the man who is God, who lived and died and rose again. It is secondly through obedience to the teaching of Christ, which brings a confidence that God is working through his people. Finally by showing love the believer is assured of the authenticity of their Christian faith: by loving others the believer discovers the power of God at work. As a Christian believes in Christ, obeys his commands and loves others, they recognize in themselves, and others see it too, that here is a person born of God.

1 John 4:1–3

Recognize falsehood

In a world where many tell us how to live we are reminded to be discerning and to trust only those who teach that Jesus Christ is both God and became a human being.

If you were the devil, how would you go about undermining the church? How would you set about destroying God's people? How about a little twisting of the message so it sounds plausible but is not the truth of the gospel? Have a few ministers of your own, looking like authentic ministers of the gospel, sounding spiritual and exciting, and able to gently and subtly move believers away from their faith without them realizing what is happening. Throw in some signs and wonders – people always follow the sensational and spectacular. They are eager to believe the dramatic rather than think through whether something is true and fits with what is known about God and Christ and their purposes. A bishop would be good. Make him a very clever bishop, but so muddle up his intellect and spiritual understanding that he no longer believes in the important things like the resurrection, isn't sure about the virgin birth, and actually isn't sure about God at all.

If only this were a humorous fiction. But it isn't. False teachers and prophets have proclaimed a false gospel in every generation. That is why John says that we should be discerning and must not think that everyone who claims to speak the truth is actually speaking the truth.

In the contemporary Christian world, where tape ministries are widely available, where there are many Christian conferences, Christian radio, Christian magazines as well as the wider secular media, we need to be discerning. We need to test the spirits. We dare not believe every persuasive speaker that comes along.

In these few verses there is a command to follow and a test to administer. First the command: a simple request to test those who come to teach, 'do not believe every spirit, but test the spirits' (verse 1). In the time of John, as now, many false prophets were to be found. There are so many who seek our attention, our support and our commitment, claiming to have an answer or the answer to anything and everything.

At the time this letter was written there were evil spirits prevalent in the culture of the day: those who claimed to be speaking with the voice of God, claiming special powers, abilities and experiences, offering all manner of spiritual or material rewards, and yet who were false teachers, evil guides, leading the undiscerning away from God rather than closer to God. As Christians, many of us live in complacent ignorance of the devil's schemes to undermine the work of Christ and the church. We don't therefore recognize false teaching, particularly when it is subtly counterfeit and is the truth reinterpreted in a bogus way.

There are those who come to us appearing superspiritual. These seemingly spiritual giants tell us that if only we have enough faith and pray effectively we will not suffer. They suggest only the ungodly suffer; only the faithless are sad or in pain. They claim it is evidence of lack of trust in God if you are in difficulty.

I remember being in a Christian community where the

wife of one of the leaders died suddenly and unexpectedly. She was in her thirties with a young family. As we were led in worship we were not permitted to grieve, to feel sad or to weep. We were exhorted to rejoice and worship because God had taken this young woman to heaven. We were forced to repress natural human emotions of grief and loss and expected to achieve some artificial spiritual state where we did not grieve or feel sadness but only rejoiced in the Lord.

The so-called superspiritual might deny the importance of natural human reactions, of bereavement, pain and suffering; they can be cruel and thoughtless in their words. Some say suffering is illusory; pain only appears in the absence of faith. Since the flesh is nothing and the Spirit is everything, we should not suffer, in body or mind. Other versions of such false teaching include the idea that prosperity is what God promises us. God's people should only know good times and blessing; difficulties and problems are of the flesh. If you pray enough and believe enough you won't be poor or have problems.

These and other false teachings are cruel and malicious falsehoods for those who go through painful trials. They are wrong and yet they have an appearance of truth. They cause hurt and can be hugely damaging teachings for many. We are God's people, we are called to follow the path of suffering as Christ did, we are commanded to be a people who experience all the trials and difficulties of life in the flesh. We are to follow the example of Christ who is God and was a person with all the associated frailties.

False teaching such as this is cruel because it falsely blames people at their most difficult times of life. In the long term it denies believers the opportunity of knowing God's grace through the trials of life. God's people are denied the full joy and hope of the transforming power of Christ. It is hard to cope with the difficulties of today; it is even harder when it is denied that those difficulties actually exist, or when the sufferer is accused of being responsible for their own suffering.

We are susceptible to false teaching because in one form

or another it panders to the way we would like things to be rather than the way God has provided. Wrong teaching appeals to our desire for an easier life and the comfort zone. In essence, false teaching seeks to change the words of Jesus from 'small is the gate and narrow the road that leads to life' (Matthew 7:14) to making it a wide gate and a more comfortable path.

Many of the false teachings around are like sweets. They taste good, but they rot the teeth. So much of what we hear that is a human version of the truth may sound good, but it rots the soul. God expects us to be discerning.

Having given a command to test the spirits, John then goes on to tell his readers how to do it, how to check that those teaching are from God. The evidence for the validity or otherwise of their teaching is discovered in what they say about Christ. Do they confess that Jesus was both man and God, that God humbled himself to death on a cross and rose again? The background to the problem for the Christians of Ephesus, to whom this letter was probably sent, was that there were those preaching that Christ did not come in the flesh, that it was not Christ on the cross, but the man Jesus of Nazareth. They believed that the heavenly 'Christ' departed from the earthly Jesus just before the crucifixion. Their view of the flesh was that it was evil and God could not have demeaned himself by suffering and going through the humiliation of being on the cross.

This teaching is not only wrong, but it is also seriously flawed in its consequences. If flesh is evil and we deny that the Son of God ever came in human bodily form, then Jesus Christ can never be our pattern or example (1 Peter 2:21; Philippians 2:5). Neither can he be the high priest who opens the way to God. The true high priest must be like his people in all ways. He must know our weakness and temptations (Hebrews 2:17). If Jesus was not human then he was unable to identify with us. Furthermore, Jesus cannot be our saviour. To save people he had to be one with us. He had to know human experience and identify with the ones he came to save. If he was not human, then we deny the body can ever be the temple of the Holy Spirit (1 Corinthians 6:19). Finally, if we deny the incarnation, we deny that there can be any real union between God and people. If spirit is all together good and the body is evil, then God and humanity can never be in relationship. The great truth of the incarnation is that God became flesh so that there might be a real relationship between God and his people.

For John, as for the other New Testament writers, it is crucial that the Son of God is acknowledged as coming in the flesh. Those who fail to accept the humanity of Christ or teach contrary to this are false guides and are actually from the antichrist. Such strong words are necessary because the issue is so serious. Earlier in this letter (2:18), when John also writes about the antichrist, I attempted to explain something of who that term refers to. John calls antichrists those who come pretending to be from God and claiming to have the gospel message, who are in fact charlatans and impostors. The message they deliver does not result in the transforming power of the gospel in people's lives, but only delivers division and discord.

Questions

1. In what circumstances should the church test the teaching of those within the fellowship? Why might this be difficult when different personalities and other issues are involved?
2. How can we be more discerning in our personal relationships with people, both Christians and non-Christians? Why is this important? How can lack of discernment in friendship cause problems?
3. What do you consider to be the most dangerous teaching currently around? It might be the absence of any absolutes as argued by contemporary culture, or the way the church has sold out to Western values, unable to differentiate between the gospel and a Western way of living, or something else.

4. Invent an attractive gospel. What would be really 'good news', which people would like to hear? In what ways does it differ from the truth?

The anointing of the Holy Spirit

John confidently affirms that the Holy Spirit is at work in and through those to whom he writes. He knows that those who belong to Christ have received the gift and anointing of the Holy Spirit to enable them to serve God, to be witnesses to Christ and to live the transformed life that is theirs now they have been forgiven.

In recent decades 'the anointing of the Holy Spirit' has sparked debate and differences of opinion. There are many views on how the Holy Spirit works within the believer and many different experiences of the Holy Spirit. There is a diversity amongst Christians, and God through the Holy Spirit deals with each believer according to his purposes and the individual's need.

All Christians are filled with the Holy Spirit. We cannot be Christians without God's Holy Spirit being at work in us (Romans 8:9). It is the work of the Holy Spirit that enabled us to become Christians in the first place. The Holy Spirit lives within all believers (2 Timothy 1:14). However, it is possible for us to quench the Holy Spirit and to resist his work in our lives (1 Thessalonians 5:19). Being anointed with the Holy Spirit is an essential part of being a Christian, but it is necessary to keep on being filled with God's Spirit (Ephesians 5:18) on a regular basis so that we might have God's strength for living holy and transformed lives.

The issue of the anointing of the Holy Spirit has sadly caused much controversy and debate. Some have argued that it is a 'second blessing' following conversion. Others have argued you must speak in tongues if you are full of the Holy Spirit. The New Testament teaches that to know

Christ and to serve him we need the Holy Spirit; we cannot do anything alone (John 15:5). The Holy Spirit may give some a dramatic and amazing postconversion experience and they may speak in tongues. Others may not receive the gift of tongues but receive other gifts to use for the benefit of the body of Christ. All Christians will have God's power to resist evil, to witness and show the love of Christ, to be discerning and wise, and to serve the kingdom of God.

In his letter John is most concerned that the Christians he writes to understand that their anointing with the Holy Spirit means that they are taught the truth and led into all the fullness of understanding of God and his purposes in Christ that they need (for example 2:20 and 2:27). John's emphasis in referring to the anointing of the Holy Spirit is that the Holy Spirit brings truth and wisdom about issues that require spiritual discernment.

It almost seems here that John is arguing against the need for his own writing. If the Spirit leads them into all truth, then isn't John redundant? Not so! John's writing and teaching is necessary. It is through his writing that the believers are led into truth. As they reflect on the Apostle's teaching, it is the Holy Spirit who brings understanding about differing ideas and guides the believers into truth as they trust and obey him.

Stop and think: Discernment

Discernment is important for Christians today. So many different influences and arguments come to us presenting plausible claims. There are so many potential courses of action that wisdom to recognize what is right and what is the leading of the Holy Spirit is essential. Churches have died or been seriously distracted by misleading personalities and ideas. The ability to discern God's will and the ability to discern when it is not God at work is crucial and should be emphasized.

Discernment is sound judgment: an ability given by God to distinguish between what is right and what is wrong, what is good and what is evil. Discernment can be gained through reading God's word and through a renewed mind. It is in the regular reading of the Bible that the message of life in Christ becomes clearer and the individual Christian can exercise greater discernment when facing issues that require a judgment to be made. All Christians are encouraged to have their minds renewed and transformed by the Holy Spirit so that they think and respond in a godly Christ-centred way (Romans 12:2).

In the New Testament, discernment is a gift given to some believers in particular, by the Holy Spirit, in order to judge between spirits in the community of believers (1 Corinthians 12:10). However, all Christians are encouraged to be discerning and exercise sound judgment and not to be gullible or susceptible to the deceptions of Satan.

Discernment isn't just needed in community decisions and deliberating about the content and emphasis of teaching, as is the main focus of the letters of John. It is required by the individual to perceive what is right for them and what is not. Paul reminds us (Philippians 1:9–10) that we need discernment in order to know what it is best to do and to be pure and blameless. Discernment also involves not judging by outward appearances, understanding the significance of events (Matthew 24:32–33), and being able to rule and lead effectively (Proverbs 8:14–16).

▶ Discuss occasions when you or people close to you have most been aware of needing discernment. Why is discernment at times a problem for us?

▶ What guidelines would you suggest to a young Christian who was trying to discern God's will for her life?

▶ How can we discern God's mind about global events such as the terrorist attack on the World Trade Centre in New York in September 2001?

1 John 4:4–6

On the winning side

**For all Christians there are times when the opposition
appears crushing. However, in every circumstance the
believer has the power of God to rely on, who is greater
than any other authority or influence of any kind.**

It would have been sobering for those
who received this letter to be reminded
that the opposition is so active. To have
it spelt out that without care and discernment they could be distracted and led away from the
gospel truth is not a comfortable issue to face. However,
John does not leave it there. He does not leave his audi-
ence in any doubt spiritually or insecure in their faith; he
delivers powerful words to encourage and inspire them.
As the caring and concerned pastor, he seeks not only to
warn and teach, but also to encourage and inspire.

He moves on from the opposition they face and gives
the believers encouragement that they can tackle any
opposition with confidence. He is unequivocal in his comments: 'You, dear children, are from God and have overcome them, because the one who is in you is greater than
the one who is in the world' (verse 4). Not 'you might' or
possibly or maybe: no vagueness, ambiguity or uncertainty. John builds up the conviction and esteem of his
people by reinforcing whose side they are on and emphasizing who has the victory. He affirms that they are from
God. We all need to hear someone say that to us at times
of stress and pressure. We need reassurance that God is at
work in our lives. When we face difficulties or opposition
that threatens to overwhelm us, we need to know that
God's grace is still there sustaining us.

It is not so different today, as far as false teachers are concerned, as it was in the first century. God's people today are still under attack. It may be false prophets who claim a spirituality of half-truths that are actually untruths. It may be the latest views of free thinkers and liberals that threaten the gospel truth by compromising God's absolutes and broadcasting a message of complete toleration of everything, including sin and evil. Many Christians face the false teaching of relativism and materialism on a daily basis: the idea that nothing is of ultimate value, that no religion can claim to be the truth – it is only truth for those who believe it to be so, or the thinking that only what you can know through the senses is actually true and all else is open to interpretation.

It is very easy to be intimidated by others; their knowledge may seem so broad, their confidence so overwhelming and their arguments so persuasive. It is easy to be impressed by the lifestyle and convictions of others, such as those who live for the gods of pleasure, possessions and promotion. Their philosophy looks so convincing. Many people may have fascinating and novel ideas about God and Jesus. They may make you feel very uncomfortable and you may not necessarily know how to argue against them. Some scientists mock our faith and suggest we should get on with something more useful than worship and faith in Christ. They make a good case for rational argument and empirical understanding.

All of these adversaries might seem so crushing. John reminds his readers, as he reminds us, that they have overcome those false teachers who tried to distract and disturb them. Ancient Ephesus was an amazing mixture of philosophies and 'isms', all trying to attract followers. In addition, it was a powerful centre of occult and magic practices, and of secret mystery cults with orgiastic worship. But John repeats his exhortation that they have nothing to worry about, no concerns that should undermine their confidence in Christ. Then we have those glorious words of hope, confidence and faith: 'the one who is in you is greater than the one who is in the world' (verse

4). Jesus Christ in them, through the power of the Holy Spirit, is so much more powerful than the antichrist and all his agents. They need not fear or be in doubt because it is the God of the universe who indwells them, giving them all the resources they need to resist the power, teaching and disruptive influences of false teachers.

The force of these words was brought home to me again just recently. A young mother, new to our church, had requested an opportunity to talk. She is a Christian from the Philippines, married with a young daughter. Her background in the Philippines was in a context where superstition and evil spirits were prevalent. She has friends who are involved with black magic and witchcraft. These friends have held sway over her so much so that, although she knows the transforming power of God in her life, she has also been the victim of panic attacks and severe fear and anxiety about evil spirits, spells and demons. As we talked together we reflected on this verse and it was inspiring to see how these words gave her hope, strength, confidence and assurance.

The context that John wrote in would have been much more akin to the world that my Philippine friend knows than the world many of us inhabit in churches in developed nations. Occasionally we catch a glimpse of the forces of evil and malevolent powers that would seek to undermine us and destroy God's work, but more often we are blind to their activities and succumb to their strategies unwittingly. These words are a great encouragement to all of us that, whatever our situation, whatever opposition we face as God's people, his power at work in us is much greater in every way than any other power that may threaten us.

The opposition, however it appears, can seem so devastating. It can seem to dwarf and floor us. But when we look at those giants in the true light, we see they are only shadows. Children can often be terrified by the shadow of a huge monster on the wall, ten times bigger than they are, until they realize that the monster is just a tiny toy silhouetted in a lamp, which casts a scary but powerless image.

The devil is like that with his attempts to overturn the truth. He seeks to stand in the way of the Light. His interference and attempts to undermine the work of Christ cast huge shadows, but that is all they are; they have no substance or reality. With faith in the work of Christ and a discerning Spirit at work within us, we will overcome the evil one because Christ's power is at work in us and that power is much greater than any power that the devil might have.

In verse 5, John outlines the context in which the Christians in Ephesus find themselves. They are meeting and engaging with those whose worldview is not centred on Christ, although it has an appearance of spirituality. Since they are from the world and not centred on Christ, they speak and teach only from the viewpoint of the world. They speak in ways that are attractive and appealing. They say what the world wants to hear, but it is not the gospel truth of Jesus Christ. The devil has won a minor skirmish in the battle that he lost when Jesus died and rose again. The attractive teaching has persuaded some and distracted them from the truth of the gospel.

This section of the letter concludes with the simple understanding that those who belong to Christ have a hunger for the truth and those who do not belong to Christ desire other things. They wish to have their ears full of falsehood, for they are deceived and in darkness and unable to recognize their vulnerable state.

Questions

1. Discuss the circumstances when you need reassurance that the Spirit who lives in you is greater than the spirit who lives in the world. Why do we at times feel defeated by greater powers?
2. Reflect on the following verses and consider how they can help when it appears that the opposition is overwhelmingly powerful: Isaiah 41:10; Romans 8:28; Romans 8:31–39; 2 Corinthians 12:9–10; Philippians 4:13.

3. Does the church give in too readily to false teaching, for
   example in South Africa where for so many years the
   church co-operated with apartheid, or in Hitler's
   Germany where the church conspired with a treacher-
   ous government? Where do you see such dangers
   today?

1 John 4:7–16a

God is love

Love is the essence of faith as love is the essence of God.

Love spelt out (verses 7–12)

Having spoken of the requirement to
love each other if we are living in the
light (2:10), and then having emphasized the way God
lavishes his love upon us (3:1), in this section John articu-
lates fully the theme of love. Love is the essence of God
and that is why it is so crucial for those who claim the
name of Christ to seek to live in this love and allow themselves to be channels of it.

John appeals again to his people to 'love one another'.
He knows that there is nothing that can defeat love. Love
is the most powerful and effective way of making Christ
known to others. So many are attracted to Christian faith
when the love of Christ is evident, but our instinct and
nature is to be unloving. Our instinct is to look after our
own interests. When we are born of God and know the
love that God has shown for us, then we can take that love
and show it to others. Much more than that, when we are
born of God, then the love of God is recreated in our lives:
a bit like being given a genetic disposition towards love.

In a family of great musicians, often the children will have an aptitude for music. Partly because they are surrounded by music all the time, but also because they have received in their physical make-up from their parents a talent for music. Similarly, in a household of sporting prowess, often the children will get from their parents the physique, personality or co-ordination that makes them able to do well at sports. We should not be surprised then when we are born of God that the character of God is found in us. As we are reborn of God then we find the Holy Spirit at work within us, increasingly making us to reflect God's love.

As we have already said in commenting on 1 John 3:16–18, love is about actions; it is about doing practical things when there is a need, it is about showing compassion and supporting each other. It includes being tolerant of each others' differences; it is about being understanding and forgiving.

Love is the heart of the Christian message: when all is stripped away, when we go back to sources and starting points, it is all about love. God created the world and the universe because he wanted to show his love and wanted to be in a relationship of love with those who could freely respond to him. Everyone it seems believes in love. Every religion, every ideology, every political party, every creed approves of love. This means it is very easy to be in love with the idea of love without ever discovering what true love is or living a life of love.

During the hippy era, the Beatles song 'All you need is love' was very popular. People knew, as they frequently know today, that it is all they need, but they don't know where it comes from. They have the idea but not the power to love. They settle for a poor imitation and go to the wrong place to get it.

The love spoken of in John's letter is not sexual attraction. Its not the affection we might feel for family or country, or a love born out of loyalty. It is not the friendship love of two mutually supportive people. The love talked of here is unconditional love: love that gives without expecting anything in return. It is love that follows Christ's example of laying down his life for others. It means leaving aside all wish for appreciation, for applause and approval, all the desire to receive credit or recognition. It is being willing to adopt the role of the servant, to accept lack of honour. Love is informed and concerned.

So much that is thought of as love today is simply a shallow, sentimental response to a situation that is sad or demanding. It is an unthinking response that costs little to the giver and achieves little to change the situation. I am reminded of the outpouring of 'love' and grief at the death of Diana, Princess of Wales. She was a beautiful icon of Western culture, tragically killed in a car accident in Paris in August 1997. If it were a deep meaningful love, would it not have led to change rather than just thousands of flowers lining the streets?

Martyn Lloyd-Jones remarked that 'love in action is highly intelligent'. It doesn't act hastily or superficially; it seeks genuine responses and help for a situation. Love in action is not a trivial response. Love thinks, puts itself in the position of the other person, and is imaginative, ingenious and inventive. Love finds a way of overcoming evil with good. It is without pretence, without wanting to gather a good reputation for being loving.

For some of us it takes a long time before we take love seriously. Maybe trials, or the difficulties of life, soften our harsh ways and reorder our priorities. If we are authentic in our faith the day has to come when we take our need to love seriously, not just talk about it or romance about it, but show genuine Jesus-love.

I work in a church where God is moving in significant ways. Our membership and congregations are growing and there is an expectancy and enthusiasm for God's community. Even so, there are situations that seemingly defeat us. When we have done everything we can for someone practically, have exhausted all the wisdom that God has given us for them, what do we do? We love them. It is hard. Love is not the easy path; it is the tough path. It is the path of pain and disappointment, but also the path of hope, of eternity, of new life.

In the final analysis love is the only response we can make to a God who has loved us so much that he has made us his children, lavishing his love on us. It is the only response we have to a world in blindness; our love should be a beacon shining out in the darkness. It is the only response of a grateful heart when we realize all that is ours in Christ: our freedom to be like him, to be holy, to be righteous, to have life, to have assurance, to have confidence before God himself.

We talk so readily about love and yet find it so difficult to actually love in practice. Our motivation to love is undermined, through tiredness, busyness or simply because we don't find people loveable. The inspiration to love others, when it is difficult, comes from the love God has shown us. Our desire to love must come from God himself, his example and his power at work within us.

John makes the seemingly curious comment that 'no-one has ever seen God' (verse 12). The point is that when we love then, although we might not see God physically, his presence is made complete amongst us. John 1:18 raises this point: 'No one has ever seen God, but God the One and Only, who is at the Father's side, has made him known.'

The most powerful evangelistic tool that the church has is the love of God. Almost everyone wants to be loved. A community that shows love to all who join or visit will have a great impact for the kingdom of God. So often Christian fellowship is characterized by division and disagreement rather than love. Love is the goal to be aimed at; it is the foundation of our lives together in Christ.

Being certain of unseen things (verses 13–16a)

John returns to the theme of assurance of life in Christ (verses 13–15). In 1 John 3:24 he has already made the point that we know we belong to him because the Holy Spirit he gave us lives within us. John considers it worth reinforcing that his readers can know that their relation-ship with God is authentic because of the Spirit they have received.

Let us remind ourselves that this is a community of believers who have been told by false teachers that they have got it wrong, that they need special knowledge and understanding, that Christ didn't come in the flesh because God is too spiritual for that. The believers had had their faith seriously undermined and needed reassurance and frequent reminders that they were living in the truth and that they could be confident in their faith.

So many today who are Christians find their faith threatened and their confidence in their standing before God weakened by the comments of others and the influences of those around. Whenever our relationship with God is under attack and we are tempted to doubt the grace of our Lord in our lives and wonder if we really do belong to God's people, then this verse instructs us to remember all that the Holy Spirit has done in our lives. It is not a bad idea to take time to reflect on all that God has done for us, and the ways in which God's Spirit is working and has worked in our lives. Our assurance and confidence will be built up and our response to God will be greater.

Moving on to verse 14, John slips in a seemingly common and obvious comment about Jesus the Saviour of the world. It is not popular today to claim that anyone is the unique anything; that is regarded as arrogant and bigoted. The issue for us as God's people is that is what we believe, that there is only one way to God and that is through Jesus Christ. This was an encouragement to the first-century Christians when everything seemed to be going wrong and they were struggling with those who criticized and condemned them. It is also an encouragement to us who believe that whatever the world might criticize us for or might suggest is lacking in our perspectives, we believe, and have the affirmation of the Holy Spirit to support us, that Christ is from God and he is the way of salvation.

John takes us back to basics in verse 15. Anyone who accepts that Jesus of Nazareth is the Christ sent by God has God within them. The imagery here is of being full of and surrounded by the presence and love of God. So overwhelming and completely encapsulating is the presence of God in and around the believer, that it can only be described as being like water on a hot day, that both fills and refreshes you from the inside and cleanses and rejuvenates you on the outside.

Since the sense of God's presence is so powerful and so overwhelming, John concludes this paragraph by a summary thought. Due to all that has been said, God's love, his Spirit and his overwhelming presence, we know he is there for us, we can rely on his love, we can be confident of the hope we have no matter what the false teachers and misguided influences are saying.

Questions

1. Why is the church so rarely thought of as a community of love? What practical things can you do to encourage love in your church?
2. Encourage one another by remembering how in recent days, months or years you have been aware of God's Holy Spirit at work within you.
3. Can all the world's problems, such as the environment, ethnic hatred and poverty, be solved through love?

1 John 4:16b–21

Fearless love

There is nothing to fear when we discover God through Jesus Christ. Jesus points us to the unconditional, self-sacrificing love of the Father.

John has not exhausted all he wishes to say on the subject of love. Even though he has already mentioned it four times in this letter (2:3–6, 3:1, 3:16 and 4:7–11), the theme of love continues to be revealed in all its depth and magnitude.

God is deeply misunderstood in our world. So many view him as an angry judge waiting to punish, or a disinterested observer who doesn't really care about the activities of the world he has created. When people discover that God is love then they wonder what love is. In human lives the fragility of love is seen. Love based on feelings, on physical attraction, on what enhances a person's image and serves their purpose is not the love of God. For many it is the only love that they know and therefore they have difficulty grasping a love that is so different and so devoid of self-interest.

Knowing that love is the key to life is not uncommon, but knowing the source of that love and discovering that love in all its depth is rare. It is easy to think that the answer to the question 'what is love?' can be found in self-help manuals or popular psychology. Many of these books do give insights and understanding, but miss out God, the source of love.

From passages such as 1 Corinthians 13 we learn the true character of love. Love is self-sacrificing, it is always there no matter what happens. It doesn't fail, it takes risks, and doesn't think about itself. True love always looks out for what is best for others and is unconditional.

In case the believers haven't yet got the message, John writes in the clearest of terms that the source of love is God: 'God is love' (verse 16b). Not God has love, not God is loving, not God is loveable, not God shows love, not God reveals love, although all of those are true; the fundamental factor that John wants his friends to grasp is that God in his very essence *is* love. His very character is love and the motivation for all his actions is love.

Again John describes believers as both being in love and love being in them. This is similar to the image of verse 15, when he spoke of God living in the believer and the believer living in God. When we open ourselves to the love of God and respond to his call on our lives to follow him and be like him, then it is his Spirit that enters us and brings us his Spirit of love so we are literally full of love and living in love. Love does not come from within ourselves. The human character, without God's help, is not capable of such love, as we are told in Mark 7:21–22: 'For from within, out of men's hearts, come evil thoughts, sexual immorality, theft, murder, adultery, greed, malice, deceit, lewdness, envy, slander, arrogance and folly.' If we do love someone with a love of our own, then it is because they have something that matters to us. We might love them for their personality, their looks, their money or the way they treat us. We can never claim that love comes from within us without any help from God. So many of our actions are loveless and selfish. We say things about others, we think things about others, we question people's motives, we cause hurt because of our lack of consideration and indifference.

We love others because of something, but God loves us because of nothing. We are all flawed human beings, we are imperfect and inadequate and yet God loves us. As it says in Romans 5:8, 'God demonstrates his own love for us in this: While we were still sinners, Christ died for us.' We cannot do anything to make ourselves more loveable but God still loves us.

Love is made complete as Christians respond to the Holy Spirit. God's original purpose in creating the world and the people of the world was that he might have someone to love and who would love him. When believers respond to Christ, God's purposes of love are being completed as believers love God and trust in him. That is why those who trust Christ can have confidence when they stand before God on Judgment Day. When Christ returns and everyone has to answer for how they have lived their lives, those who trust Christ can have confidence because God's work in their lives has been finalized and they can stand assured that they are forgiven. On Judgment Day God will see his own love in our lives; the guilt for our sin has already been taken by Christ.

The only way that God's love can be complete in our lives is if we are connected to him. The only way that we, as flawed human beings, can be linked to God is through faith in Jesus Christ as Saviour. When we respond in faith to the love of God shown in Christ, then we receive the precious gift of love through the Holy Spirit. It is the Holy Spirit who comes and allows love to flow in the barren desert of our lives and sets up a pipeline whereby the love of God can flow into us.

In this context there is nothing to fear. We need not fear God because his aim is not to trip us up or catch us out but to love us and show us his grace. So much that passes for love these days is in fact possessive and manipulative. Many children feel loved as long as they are successful, doing well at school and being a credit to their parents. If, however, they fail, and let the side down, then they fear the love of their parents, for it is then a selfish, self-seeking love not a self-sacrificing love.

If we come to God honestly and openly then there is nothing to fear, for God only wants the best for us. Love takes away that sense of fear, for when we know how much God loves us then we realize he only acts for our benefit. Our attitude to ourselves changes, because no longer do we look on ourselves as unloved human beings but we see ourselves as children loved by their heavenly

Father. We begin to understand how special we are if God gave his only Son for us.

His plan is to save us from punishment, not to punish us. Any fears we have before God, if we come in humility and in acceptance of his saving grace, are groundless. If someone lives in fear of God then they have not understood the message of hope and peace in Christ.

John concludes this chapter with a salutary reminder of the dangers of the hypocrisy of claiming to love God and not really loving at all. Let us remind ourselves again that John was writing to a community of Christians who had been under attack from those claiming to love God and to be spiritual people when they showed no love for others and caused trouble and broken relationships in the church.

John seeks to show what a nonsense this is. There is never an excuse for not showing love, if we know and understand how much God has loved us. Our love for each other comes from God and is because we know that his love for us is undeserved and generous beyond our imagination. If God's love has reached into our lives and is transforming us, then we will not hate our brother or sister. We may be disappointed by them, hurt by them, discouraged or saddened by their behaviour, but we can never hate those whom God has called to share in the kingdom of God. We may hate what they do, we may hate what they say, but to hate them is not possible if we are children of God. If we realize how much God hates our sin and rebellion and yet how deep his love is for us, then we know the example to follow in loving others.

The test of faith in Christ as Saviour and Lord is not how much you pray, how well you know your Bible, how many Christian conferences you go to or how often you attend church. The test for John is, do you confess that Jesus Christ is the Son of God who came in the flesh, fully human, and do you love your brothers and sisters in Christ? If we cannot love those into whom God has poured his love, how can we claim to love God whom we have never seen? God says 'love me, love my children'.

If only we could live this truth more effectively in our churches today. If only we could share the love of God amongst ourselves and allow love to dominate, rather than our opinions, prejudices and mistrust. So many Christians hold grudges against others; that is not the way of love. So many Christians hurt and wound others with their comments or indifference; that is not the way of love. So many ignore the needs and plight of others; that is not the way of love. We are to love each other unconditionally. We are not to base our love on whether that person fits our model of faith or has a lifestyle with which we are comfortable. We won't get any medals for loving unconditionally, as it is our Christian duty, but we will be contented in knowing God's love flowing through us if we commit ourselves to the path of love.

As we love one another we will give glory to God and we will honour him before the rest of the world. As we love each other we will honour God, and this will be a powerful witness to others and will be contagious as it gives evidence that God loves them also.

Questions

1. What are the fears that you harbour? How could God's love dispel these fears?
2. What does verse 20 have to say about those who call themselves Christians but do not love those who are also Christians? How does this verse apply in political hot spots such as Northern Ireland or South Africa?
3. Think of as many creative ways as you can of how your church community could show the love of Christ to the local area. Pray about how you might take one of the ideas and actually use it to be a witness.

1 John 5:1–5

Reborn to love

Children of God have been born to love God and each other. When they do this they are successful in overcoming the world that seems to promise so much but in fact offers so little.

The label 'born again' causes considerable derision and scorn from some quarters. The term is understood by some to mean those who are fundamentalist, anti-intellectual and narrow in their faith. Yet the image of being born again is thoroughly biblical, as we read in verse 1, and a wholly helpful metaphor for faith in Christ. To believe in Jesus Christ is to be transformed spiritually and to be born inwardly by the Spirit of God. The effect is as radical spiritually as it is physically for an unborn child to leave the womb. Believers who discover Jesus Christ and respond to his invitation to follow him leave behind the old life, centred on themselves and their own interests, and begin life centred on Christ. They are spiritual babies who have much to learn and need to grow in knowledge and understanding.

One of the words from the Bible that is frequently misunderstood is the word 'believe'. Belief is commonly understood today to mean intellectual assent or agreement. You might be asked, 'Do you believe in abortion?' People would reply either in the affirmative or in the negative, but it wouldn't make too much difference to the way they live. Even when they came across a situation of perhaps their own unplanned or unwanted pregnancy or that of a friend or family member, their beliefs about abortion in principle may be disregarded as they do what suits their situation. The New Testament concept of belief is far removed from this. Belief in the context of New Testament faith means a total commitment to Jesus Christ as Saviour and Lord. It is not just thinking, 'Yes I believe he existed and what he said is true'. It is following his teaching, trusting him, and having faith in him for every situation. It is not simply belief in the head, but a commitment of the heart, a way of life that changes our perspective on everything – our future, our careers, our attitudes and our relationships with others.

John returns to his central theme of love. Knowing that the false teachers and troublemakers have damaged relationships, the believers need to get back to good relationships, to loving each other. If they love the Father they will also love his children. This is a common sense comment. If we have love and friendship for a human father, then those sentiments will also be shared with any child of that father. Similarly, John pleads with his readers that if they love the Father, they should also love his children, each other.

At first sight John's comment in verse 2, 'we know that we love the children of God: by loving God and carrying out his commands', appears to be in conflict with what he has already said. In 3:14 John says that we know we have life because we love each other. Now, in this section of the letter, he says we know we love each other if we love God and obey his commands. The teaching is not in conflict; it is circular. Loving and obeying God and loving other believers are so closely connected that it is not possible to have one without the other. Loving God means we obey him and we love our brothers and sisters in Christ. Loving our brothers and sisters in Christ can only come from our love of God and obedience to his command. There is no inconsistency in what John is saying. God commands us to love each other, to lay down our lives for each other and to support each other, particularly in times of need.

You might think John's words in verse 3, 'This is love for God: to obey his commands. And his commands are not burdensome', are astonishing and incredible. Most of us would think that the old nature, the selfishness of sin and the pride of our hearts, makes it a battle to obey the commands of God, not something that is easy.

Maybe we have misunderstood. Possibly, obeying God and doing his will is only difficult in the anticipation of it. When we know that obeying God means, for example, apologizing to someone, we find that the hardest thing to do and yet once we set our minds and our hearts to obey God then his grace supplies the ability to do it. Then obeying God is not so difficult. The commands of God as emphasized in the first letter of John are to love each other. This can appear difficult when we consider our own inadequacies to love and the unloveliness of the person we are called to love. However, the grace of God is adequate for the situation: 'My grace is sufficient for you, for my power is made perfect in weakness' (2 Corinthians 12:9). So what appears impossible to us at the outset – our ability to obey and follow the teaching of Christ – is made attainable because of the Holy Spirit within us.

Jesus said, 'Take my yoke upon you and learn from me, for I am gentle and humble in heart, and you will find rest for your souls. For my yoke is easy and my burden is light' (Matthew 11:29). Compared to all the religious rules and regulations with which they had been burdened under the Jewish law, the commands of God in Christ are simple and uncomplicated. Obeying God's commands is not difficult because God gives the grace and the power to fulfil his will and carry out his purposes. The struggles are so often in our minds and with our fears. When we do obey, we find that obedience is the most fulfilling and satisfying way to live. When we commit ourselves to following the narrow path of life we find that God's will is 'good, pleasing and perfect' (Romans 12:2).

John goes on in verse 4 to explain more fully why obedience to God is not the burden that we at times assume it is. Obedience to God comes out of a relationship of trusting Christ. By trusting Christ, Christians have success in the struggle against the world. Christians are freed from the worldly values that cause division, envy and hatred.

Materialism, power games, ambition and status are irrelevant in Christ; they have no currency or significance. By obeying God Christians can win the battle over such issues because they are not a threat and are of no interest. The world is defeated if it has no appeal. The world only has power and influence over us as long as we are enticed and dazzled by its shallow attraction. When we see the world for what it is, in the grip of the evil one, and that all that the world offers is nothing in comparison with the riches that are ours in Christ, then there is no battle.

There is an eccentric multimillionaire named Van Hoostraten who is building himself a huge mausoleum in Sussex in the south of England. Its cost is £32 million, and its purpose is to store his art collection and his remains when he dies. This man is cold and indifferent to others. He has no interest in the children he has fathered, he doesn't believe in God, but he wants to live forever by building this mausoleum and leaving enough money to have it maintained forever. The world has ensnared him. The attraction of money, power and status have caught him and he cannot escape. He cannot fight the world, he cannot know love, and he cannot find satisfaction in his life. He thinks he is strong and powerful, that he can do anything he wants. He thinks he has defeated the world and that he will live forever. Sadly, the world, the evil one, has captured him and he will never be released from the prison he has built himself.

Those who win the battle of life and overcome the world are those who recognize that Jesus is their Saviour, that he is the Son of God and that none of these other issues are relevant. Christians have their sights set on things far superior to any this world can ever offer. The hope of the Christian is for eternity; the hope of the Christian is of a glory that the most famous human superstar can only dream of; the hope of the Christian is of life with God.

Questions

1. Why do you find obedience to God's commands difficult? Is it because you have misunderstood God's commands? What kind of faith makes them 'not burdensome'? Is 'not burdensome' here the same as 'easy'? Was it not burdensome for Jesus to obey the command in John 10:18?
2. What does it means for Christians to 'overcome the world'? Can you suggest some examples of where this has happened?
3. How should the church present Jesus as the Son of God in a context of a multifaith society? Are there wrong ways of proclaiming Jesus as the only way to the Father?

1 John 5:6–12

The testimony of God

Jesus is the Christ: the testimony of God at his Son's baptism and through the blood of Jesus' death, as well as the witness of the Holy Spirit, confirm this fact.

We live in an age where we want to be sure of things and rely on evidence and comments from others. If we go on holiday we like to hear from others that the place we have chosen is pleasant and well selected. The evidence of the brochure and holiday programmes is helpful, but the opinion of someone who has been there makes us even more confident of our choice.

In this passage we have the assurance that God himself

confirms the truth of the message that there is salvation through his Son. In these complex words about water, blood and the Spirit we come to understand how God reinforces our faith through his own testimony. Our faith is not just a matter of hope without basis. It is hope based on the evidence of God's actions. Jesus came into the world and submitted to God through water by being baptized, he gave his blood on the Cross, and the Holy Spirit is the third witness to God's actions for salvation.

Water links with baptism. Jesus was born and was baptized, and God said at his baptism, 'This is my Son, whom I love; with him I am well pleased' (Matthew 3:17). This is evidence that Jesus was human and divine, and that he came as a person to fulfil God's purposes and to be, not only the message, but also the evidence of God's plans being accomplished.

The blood is the blood that poured out of Christ on the cross. Jesus could not be the Messiah without the cross. He had to die. His death was real and necessary to make atonement for our sin.

In water and blood we are reminded that Jesus came and was baptized as a sign of his identity with humanity and yet through his blood he atoned for the sin of the world. Those who claimed he was not truly the Son of God at his baptism and death have ignored the evidence that God spoke at his baptism, when he confirmed his identity, and that the blood he provided in his death showed him to be God's perfect sacrifice.

The Holy Spirit is a witness alongside the water and the blood. The Holy Spirit also confirms the identity and importance of Jesus Christ. In the Jewish tradition two or three witnesses were required to confirm a judgment. John is confirming that Jesus has these witnesses: the water, the blood and the Spirit. Each in their different ways show that Jesus is the Messiah sent by God for the salvation of the world.

Verse 10 reminds us that for those who are Christians, who have a relationship with God through Christ, these testimonies are meaningful and helpful. For those who do not know God through Christ, these testimonies are meaningless and they reject them, making it appear that God is not true to his word. The false teachers, who do not acknowledge all that God has done in Christ, do not have the life of Christ in them and remain dead in their sins, unable to understand and grasp the glory and love available to them in Christ.

Those who have a relationship with God have the abundant life, the richest life, the fullest life possible, because their sights are not set on the shallow things of this world but on the much greater things of the spiritual realm.

Questions

1. A modern day version of denying that Jesus is God are those who genuinely believe he is a great moral teacher and place his significance alongside Gandhi or Buddha. Why is this so destructive spiritually?
2. There is a lot in this passage about God's testimony. How significant are the testimonies of Christians today in leading others to Christ? When did you last pray for an opportunity to share your testimony with others?
3. Verse 12 is clear in its statement that if someone does not believe in Jesus Christ then they will never know true spiritual life. Why is that such a difficult concept for our contemporary culture?

1 John 5:13–15

God hears but do we?

God hears us when we pray, but so often Christians find it difficult to hear what God is saying to them. Believers need to have the assurance that they can approach God about every situation.

What a great pastor John is, always focused and clear and full of hopes for his people. I wonder if we are as focused in our spiritual leadership of others, whether in a family, a small group or a congregation.

John writes so that those who believe in Christ as the Son of God might know they have eternal life. How sensitive he is in understanding that so often we can't comprehend all that is ours in Christ. We believe and yet we can't quite believe we are included. This is what John reinforces for them. They are Christians, they have the hope of eternal glory and they can have confidence in approaching God.

Confidence in approaching God would have been a new concept for these believers. Those with a Jewish background would have been brought up with the idea that God could only be approached once a year by the high priest. Everyone else was cut off by the curtain and unable to enter God's presence for themselves. Those with a Greek background would have been used to the gods being fickle and capricious. These pagan gods could only be approached through offerings and sacrifices to indulge their fragile egos.

John reminds the believers that God is not like that. God is merciful and loving and can be approached with confidence, not because we are deserving but because of

Christ opening the way between us and God. We have assurance in approaching God in prayer because God is our Father who wants to hear and answer the requests of his children.

However, verses such as these have caused us difficulties. Many faithful and committed Christians have honestly asked God for things, seeking his will, and have not received the answer that they have requested. This has led some to suggest that these verses 'don't work'. We have already begun to look at this issue when it arose earlier in the letter (3:21–22).

The crucial issue in prayer is that we listen to God's voice, follow the leading of his Spirit, and then pray in his will. So often we presume we are praying in God's will because we are asking for something that seems good. If a person has a life-threatening disease, particularly if that person is young or has a young family, then we pray earnestly that God will work a miracle, believing that that must be a good thing to happen. I think of a 26-year-old who discovered he had cancer of the liver four months before he was due to marry. It seemed so obvious to the fellowship that this young man should live, and we prayed earnestly for his healing. Sadly he died. We find it difficult to accept that a God of love would allow a young man to die in such circumstances just before his wedding. Yet we only see 'a poor reflection' (1 Corinthians 13:12); we don't see or understand the full purposes of God. Tough as some of these situations may seem to us at the moment when our grasp of eternity is imperfect, one day it will make sense and the struggles we have now will appear insignificant compared with the glory that is ours with God.

We can approach God with confidence, he is willing to hear us and listens to our cries. Just as a father does not give a child everything they ask for, and makes that child endure and persevere to build character, so God allows us to pass through difficulties for purposes we cannot understand at the present time. The important factor in prayer is to seek God and his will, knowing that often our hopes and plans are limited by a short-term vision and often a desire for a comfortable and easy time in the present.

If that sounds a little discouraging and we wonder how we can ever have faith that God will answer our prayers, never quite knowing whether or not we are praying in his will, then we should take heart. When we commit a situation to God, whether it is a marriage, examinations, a career, a house move or relationships of all kinds, we can be confident that God will act. When we ask God to pour his grace and love into people's lives, we can be assured that God works and moves. Sometimes we get it wrong when we want to determine the outcome, when we want to make God answer our prayer in a certain way. We can be sure that whenever we pray, God hears and answers. It may be that at times our enthusiasm or self-interest prevents us praying in God's will, our own will intrudes in the prayer process, and then God's answer may be 'no' or 'not yet'. This can be hard to understand when we are sure that what we are praying for is for the best. The trouble is we don't see the big picture, we just see our little corner of life in God's kingdom, and he may have much greater plans for us or those around us than we are aware of.

Questions

1. Building each other up in Christ is an essential part of fellowship and Christian community. However, many Christians feel dragged down much of the time by the constant challenge to be more holy, more obedient, more prayerful. How can we ensure there is a good balance between love, support and encouragement and the challenge to move forward in our discipleship?
2. What disappointments have you received in prayer? How have you dealt with them? Have you grown through the disappointment?
3. How can we be confident in praying for national and global issues such as violence and the environment? How can we be confident that these prayers are in God's will?

4. Put together an encouragement plan for young Christians entitled 'Confidence in God'. Look back over 1 John as you list what the essentials are in order to have a confident, joyful relationship with God.

 Stop and think: Unanswered prayer

1 John 5:14–15 makes prayer seem so simple. Yet many Christians, even those of many years' maturity, find prayer difficult. One of the issues that occurs regularly is that of unanswered prayer. We bring a situation to God many times and believe God is going to work in a certain way, but after maybe years of prayer it seems that God does not answer us.

There are many reasons and explanations why it may appear that prayer has not been answered:

▶ We might not have recognized God's answer to our prayer. It may not be the answer we were expecting or hoping for, and so it seems that God has not answered when in fact he has but we haven't seen it.

▶ Often we pray for things from wrong, selfish motives (James 4:3).

▶ Sometimes we ask for things that are good but that God knows are not what are best for us. Sometimes God needs to take us through tough times and therefore says 'no' to our request for an easier path through life, to strengthen our faith and develop our character (Romans 5:1–5).

▶ Prayer may go unanswered if there are things that create a barrier between the person and God, if there is sin in the person's life (Isaiah 59:2) or disobedience (Proverbs 1:28–31). If prayer is offered to impress others or to impress God (Matthew 6:5–7), then the requests may not get very far.

Prayer is about trusting a faithful and powerful God that he will answer in the best possible way. We may doubt God when it seems that he has not answered our prayers, but we need to recognize that we have only limited understanding of a situation. Like a child who cannot understand why she has to go to bed early or must hold an adult's hand in traffic, so we don't understand why God answers 'no' or 'wait'.

There are many circumstances that we simply have to trust God for. We pray for global situations and distant issues and need to believe that God works through our prayers, but we may never know in our lifetime on earth how these prayers have been answered.

The verses in 1 John 5 encourage us to be bold and persistent in our prayers and then to trust God for the outcome. Even when we don't understand how the circumstances are evolving we still need to pray and trust God. The most difficult circumstance is when a child or young adult faces a terminal illness. For some reason that we cannot fathom at this stage of our understanding, God has a purpose in taking a young life. It is never easy to comprehend, but we should pray that we might understand that God has purposes far greater than the pain and hurt caused by the death of a dearly loved friend or family member.

▶ Is there such a thing as 'unanswered prayer' or is that a false perception of God answering in an unexpected way? Share times that you have 'felt' your prayer has been unanswered, and discuss interpretations of such times other than that your prayer has not been answered.

▶ Think of times when God has graciously not answered your prayer in the way that you might have hoped. These may be unwise prayers for yourself or those you love, or prayer asking God to give you something or a role that would have been unhelpful to you.

1 John 5:16–21

Keep yourself from sin

John finishes his letter by reinforcing the need to deal with the problem of sin, and by emphasizing the truth of Jesus Christ as the Son of God and the importance of avoiding anything that might take our devotion from Christ.

If we see a brother or sister in Christ do wrong, is our immediate response to pray for them? More often than not we gossip about them, judge them, draw all manner of conclusions about their wrongdoing, and generally revel in their downfall. That says more about our prejudices and lack of genuine love for each other than anything about the person who has done wrong. John's teaching to us is that if we see a Christian doing wrong then we should pray for them. It is easy to criticize or talk about them, but John expects us to do the best for them, which is to pray.

The more difficult comment of John's in these verses is concerning 'a sin that leads to death' (verse 16). What is this sin? Frequently anxious believers worry that they have committed the sin that leads to death and there is therefore no hope for them. John had in mind those who had tasted of the grace of God and known his salvation and then rejected it. Through arrogance or pride they assumed that they knew better than God does. This is the sin leading to death, because those who have rejected God have rejected life. And rejecting God (see 2:19) means rejecting and leaving the church. Those who are anxious that they might have committed the sin that leads to death are unlikely to be guilty of such a sin. Those who have been guilty of such a sin are not anxious and don't care that they have rejected the life God has offered them, which they have tasted. Those who are concerned about God cannot be those who are without hope of life.

John in writing this letter had in mind the false teachers who had tried to lead astray the faithful followers of Christ. It was them that John was thinking of when he spoke of 'sin that leads to death'. It was the denial of Jesus Christ as the fully human and divine Son of God and the denial of him as saviour of the world. Those who deny the gospel message and seek to persuade others to reject the good news of salvation in Christ are the ones who put themselves beyond the life that is found in believing in God and in Christ as his Son.

In the final three verses of this letter John returns to a number of themes that he has already addressed. He wants to summarize previous thoughts and make sure that his readers have really got the message.

The issue of sin has been tackled several times already (1:8–10; 2:1–2; 3:4–10). But John gives one final reminder that sin and the believer do not belong together. Those who are in the family of God through belief in Jesus Christ do not intentionally sin. Their whole desire is to be like Christ himself: to be loving, holy and innocent. Christians fail at times, but that is not their intention or yearning. Christians are helped in their fight against sin by being protected by God, so that the devil cannot get at them as he can at those who are outside of God's protection. As God's people we all struggle with weaknesses in our lives, with thoughts, words and behaviours that disappoint God and for which we need forgiveness. Our aim must be to defeat sin in our lives. Not to accept it is as part of life, but to earnestly seek to rid ourselves of those things that fall far short of God's perfection. As one preacher put it, 'Christians are not sinless, but they do sin less.'

In verse 19 John reminds us that as Christians we belong to God but we live in a world that is still, for the time being, under the control of evil. In the following two verses he reminds his readers again of the truth of what they believe and, without specifying, he is showing the error of the false teachers who have wreaked such havoc amongst them. The Son of God has come, Jesus Christ himself. Remember the opening verses of this letter, where the writer exclaims, 'which we have heard, which we have looked at and our hands have touched' (1:1). John can speak so confidently of knowing because he knew Jesus in human form. He is now in Christ as a believer and all of this confirms to him the truth of God revealing himself in Christ and the eternal life that is available through him.

The final comment of this letter is strange: 'keep yourselves from idols', or 'keep away from anything that might take God's place in your heart'. There are no best wishes, no closing greetings, no looking forward to seeing you soon. The last words are keep yourself from false devotion. John recognizes the danger for all of us. It is so easy to abandon what is real and be taken in by what is false.

In Ephesus this was a particular problem. The Temple of Diana was a powerful pagan influence over the whole city. One of the philosophers of the time spoke of the temple being the darkest of places, where morals were worse than those of beasts and where behaviour of the vilest kind occurred. The Christians John wrote to were living in this context: a society sold out to powers of darkness and evil. This verse tells them that Christians must keep from such things. To get on in business or in other fields of society it might have been important to go along with idol worship. John is unequivocal – have nothing to do with it. Shun idols of any sort; they are a sham. Focus only on Christ; allow your devotion and worship to go to no other.

Christians today must keep away from anything that might take God's place in our lives and priorities. The devil is so subtle and sometimes we don't even realize we have given our heart to something else until it is a complete wrench to give it up. The command here is clear: we must keep ourselves separate from worshipping anything other than Christ.

It can happen so easily. Ambition, family, relationships, personal fulfilment – all these things can take the place of

Christ. We can put them above our worship of our Lord; we can put them above our commitment to serve him above all others. We justify it to ourselves by saying what we are doing is good, it's helping others, it's my right. We need to make sure that it is Christ first and these other things follow on, and not Christ at the end of the priorities.

Questions

1. How seriously does your Christian community take its responsibility to pray for those who sin, and to support and discipline those who struggle with a particular sin in their lives? Do we have a tendency to 'brush sin under the carpet'?
2. What are the main forms of idolatry found in our contemporary culture? Are Christians as likely as anyone else to be found giving their allegiance to them?
3. If a person was deeply troubled by verse 16, thinking that they had committed 'a sin that leads to death', how would you support and counsel them?

The unforgivable sin

Christians in every generation have been anxious in case they have committed the 'unforgivable sin'. For those of a tender conscious or new to faith, it is common to be troubled by the possibility of being guilty of a sin for which there is no forgiveness.

Does such a sin exist?

1 John 5:16 refers to a sin that leads to death, implying that having committed this sin it is not possible to be forgiven or to have true life in Christ. Matthew 12:31–32 and Hebrews 10:26–29 speak of an attitude of the will that

creates such a barrier between the person and God that the person has put themselves beyond God's grace. These verses, along with other similar passages, speak of the determined slander of the Holy Spirit or when the works of Jesus Christ and the Holy Spirit are attributed to the power of Satan, making a further mockery of Jesus. It is a defamatory accusation that comes without remorse and in an arrogance of spirit that can put the person beyond the workings of the Holy Spirit. (Note that Matthew 12:31–32 is a warning to the Pharisees mentioned in Matthew 12:24 and not a pronouncement of judgment on them.)

This is a difficult idea for many in a culture where God's grace is emphasized and the truth that nothing is able to separate us from the love of God (Romans 8:39) is such a spiritual anchor. Nothing outside of ourselves can separate us from God, but we can put ourselves outside of God's grace. If a person has experienced God's grace and has known the truth of the gospel and then denies it, they are in effect calling God a liar and Jesus Christ a fraud.

Those who disregard God in his love, holiness and power, without remorse or regret, have chosen the path of death and have rejected the path of life. We need the reminder that God is a God of grace, but he is also a God of judgment for those who do not respond to his love.

Might I have committed the unforgivable sin?

If someone is concerned that they might have committed this sin, then it most unlikely that they have. To have committed the unforgivable sin is not to care or be concerned about the consequences. It is to have such a hardness of heart and indifference or hatred to all that is good that they would have no sensitivity to having hurt or saddened God. This is not a sin of omission, something we do wrong by default by not doing the right thing. Neither is it a sin of ignorance. It is not something we can do without realizing it or because we are unsure of what it is. It is a wilful rejection of God's love and grace, knowing what that love and grace are.

HOLD ON TO THE TRUTH AND CARE FOR GOD'S WORKERS

2 John and 3 John

Stop and look

John's second letter

The books of the Bible can be something of a mystery to us if we don't have a little background information to help us on our way. It may strike you as a little strange that the second letter of John appears in our New Testament. It is a real letter, written by a real person about a real situation.

Let us look briefly at who wrote the letter and who he wrote it to. Then we will consider when it was written, and finally why it has become part of our New Testament and is considered to be the word of God.

As we saw when we looked at 1 John, all three letters bearing John's name are thought to have been written by the Apostle John. The Apostle John spent the last years of his life in the area of Ephesus, and the letters he wrote were sent to Christian communities in Asia Minor, of which Ephesus was a part, with which he was in contact. This particular letter, 2 John, was written to an unnamed Christian community, possibly keeping the location and name discrete because there was persecution of Christians at that time.

The letter, like the other two letters of John, was most likely written towards the end of the first century, around AD 90, when Christians were facing considerable opposition and persecution throughout the Roman Empire.

The letter was written because there were specific issues that needed to addressed. John wanted his friends to be informed and reminded of the basis of their faith in the light of false teachers and a temptation to drift away from the love and truth that their Saviour Jesus Christ taught.

John's third letter

This third letter was most likely written by the same

person who wrote the first two letters and the Gospel of John. Christian tradition indicates that it was the Apostle John. It covers the themes that John is most associated with such as love and false teachers and is in his style of writing. This is a slightly unusual letter for the New Testament in that it was written to a personal friend. Many, but not all, of the New Testament letters were written to communities of Christians. This letter was written to a friend about issues that were of concern. It was written at a time when the Christian faith was about 60 years old, around AD 90, and some problems with leadership and visiting preachers were becoming apparent.

It may seem a little odd that a personal letter should find its way into the New Testament. The church leaders who finally decided what should be considered the word of God and therefore part of the New Testament had a number of criteria to guide them. Letters and documents were accepted if:

▶ They had apostolic authorship.

▶ They reflected the truth that Jesus taught and did not contradict any of the teaching of Jesus.

▶ The message of the document was of interest and applied to the whole church, not just a specific situation.

▶ It had been helpful in some way to the church to have the document.

In this way it was discerned which writings had been penned under the influence of the Holy Spirit and were significant for the basis and integrity of the teaching of the church in every age.

2 John 1–6

Back to basics: love and truth

Love and truth are essential central themes of the gospel. Christians need to be people who love and live in the truth.

The message of this letter is practical. It reflects the warmth and interest of an older leader concerned for the well being of his friends. It focuses on those crucial features of Christian living, truth and love. Both themes are emphasized and reinforced so that the believers might be united and strong when threatened by division and disunity.

The opening three verses are a conventional letter greeting, although with a veiled reference to the actual identity of the recipients. 'The chosen lady and her children' is likely to be a symbolic image referring to a local church community. It is a warm and friendly greeting. Today we might write to a fellowship 'from a senior friend to the honourable couple and their children'. It is a delicate and affable greeting to close acquaintances who are most likely those who gather in the name of Christ in the local community around Ephesus.

John is open and genuine in his expression of love to his readers. He is not embarrassed or afraid of being thought weak by showing that he feels deeply for their relationship together. Often the Apostles have an image of godly distance and spiritual formality. Nothing could be further from the truth as John conveys his thoughts with affection and sincere attachment to his readers.

John gives great emphasis to the truth in these opening greetings. This reminds us of the words in John's Gospel about truth spoken by Jesus: 'You will know the truth, and the truth will set you free' (John 8:32). The truth is liberating and life generating, and the truth is Jesus, human and divine, Saviour and Lord.

Just a couple of weeks ago a young woman came to our church and requested prayer. I soon discovered as I talked with her that she had been converted 7 months earlier from Islam and just that weekend her family had become aware of her new-found faith. She was staying away from home until she knew how safe she would be. The amazing testimony of this young woman was how the truth had set her free. She felt after many years of being burdened and oppressed by religion that now she had discovered the truth and the sense of liberty was astounding. Those of us who take for granted the freedom we have sometimes fail to recognize quite how much the truth of Jesus Christ releases us. It is this truth that binds us together as God's people and holds us in unity, whatever our background and circumstances.

In verse 3 the apostle follows the greeting with a three-fold blessing and encouragement. He reminds his readers of the grace, mercy and peace that are theirs in Christ.

Grace is God's help to us when we are helpless, his generosity towards us in every circumstance and situation. We don't always recognize it as such, for sometimes his grace takes us through tough experiences so that we might know him better. However, in all things God wants the best for us and acts so that we might be the best that we can be.

Mercy is God's compassion to the guilty. When we deserve judgment and punishment God deals with us with kindness; he forgives and restores. Sometimes I fear we emphasize God's grace so much that we forget just how much mercy we have received, how undeserving we are of forgiveness and eternal life, and how great is the mercy of God in granting us pardon.

Peace is God's comfort to the broken. Sin has broken and warped all of humanity. Its effect is seen in shattered relationships with each other and with God, in injustice and poverty, in evil and hatred, in selfishness and violence. God's peace brings wholeness to broken lives and to relationships that have been destroyed, and soothes the pain and suffering caused by sin. It is not a fluffy feeling. Some seem to have reduced peace to a sensation of calm and tranquillity. But God's peace is a completeness in Christ that comes from bringing all our brokenness and pain to God and allowing his healing and hope to remake us. It is a security and conviction that even in the greatest of trials and the most desperate of circumstances, God can be trusted and that his purposes are perfect.

These verses remind us of God's gifts of grace, mercy and peace coming from the essential foundation of faith, truth and love. It is easy to speak theoretically about these great spiritual themes, to talk with great authority about God's grace, mercy and peace, yet to be without love or to wander from the truth. It is sad to reflect that grace, mercy and peace can be shared or preached in a loveless and cold manner, in a context that lacks joy or warmth, in a spirit of criticism or judgmentalism. This robs these words of all love and makes it untruthful in the way it is represented.

Moving on in his thoughts John reminds us of what a thrill it is to discover that people are continuing in their discipleship, to discover that friends we haven't heard from for a while are even more committed to the truth and knowing for themselves the life that comes through Jesus Christ.

I have reached middle age, even though I have a young son who in years is not yet in double figures. We were late starters. When I meet up with friends whose children are now teenagers or in their twenties or thirties, it is a sheer delight to hear that they have taken up the gospel message for themselves. Often it hasn't been easy. There might have been turbulent times, a phase of rejecting faith and seeking other paths. There have been agonizing times for the parents as all they can do is watch and pray. Yet what a pleasure to discover that God has touched their lives and they have responded.

Love was under threat in the Christian community to which John writes because of the influence of false teachers. John implores them again to simply follow the teaching they heard from Jesus himself (John 13:34). From the beginning they have been called to love. Love involves so much. It includes respect, care, a forgiving spirit and good manners. It is also hard work, maintaining unity, welcoming strangers, listening to people's hurts, giving others the benefit of the doubt.

John sums it all up. Love is obedience to God's command, and God's command is to love. This is not an authoritarian, dictatorial type of command. It is a command born of love, motivated by love and fulfilled by love, with the purpose of generating more and more love.

Love has to be in the context of the truth about Jesus Christ to be the real thing. Any other love is a poor imitation. All other loves have a selfish aspect to them. No other love than love founded in Christ has the power to change lives and only that love is love that will last for ever. The new kingdom, when the old heaven and the old earth are gone, will be based on love; it is the eternal character of God.

Questions

1. Why is it helpful to hold together grace, mercy and peace rather than focus on just one of these themes? What might be the danger of focusing on one exclusively, for example peace, and forgetting the others?
2. Is it naive to think that love is the answer to social problems such as inner city tension or national terrorism? How could love solve such problems?
3. What can we do as churches to support each other in our discipleship and to encourage each other to hold to the faith? Are there particularly vulnerable stages of life that tend to be associated with greater possibilities for not continuing in our faith?

Divisions in the church

The church has suffered divisions within its ranks from the earliest days, through every century to the present day. Divisions arise for a variety of reasons, although Christians are called to work together for unity and to maintain unity within the fellowship (1 Corinthians 1:10). It was divisions in the church that prompted many of the New Testament letters to be written. The writers tried to advise the Christian communities on how they might respond to various divisive issues. These included the varying popularity of different leaders (1 Corinthians 1:11–12), threats from Judaizers who wanted all the Jewish regulations to be kept (Galatians 2:11–13), Gnostic teachers who added to the gospel and claimed they had a special understanding of God (1 John 4:1–3), ethnic tensions (Acts 6:1) and greed (James 4:1–3).

In the circumstances to which John wrote his letters there is a sense in which the divisions were legitimate. It is right to separate from those who hold to heresy and undermine the true gospel message (Galatians 1:6–9). In John's letters he refers to false teachers who were suggesting that it was impossible for God to take the full human form. Their teaching seriously undermined the whole gospel message. Without human form Jesus could not offer himself as an atoning sacrifice for the sin of the world.

Many of the divisions that have occurred in the church have not been over the purity of the gospel, although the Methodist, Baptist and many other traditions have their origins in a desire to be more clearly centred on the gospel message. It does seem sad that in the contemporary world there are hundreds of different denominations and church groups all believing the gospel message and seeking to live it out, but differing in style and emphasis from each other. Such a situation does not reflect well on the church and the unity that Jesus himself prayed for (John 17:11).

There are many differences of which we should be far more tolerant, for example what we eat (Romans 14:1–3). These are secondary matters about which Christians may have different opinions but which should not affect the basic unity to be found in Christ.

In the last 50 years there have probably been more divisions and separations in the church than at any other time. It is easy to see these divisions as destructive and damaging, which indeed many are, but there are occasions when a division in a church can be valuable if it gives the opportunity for further growth. The division itself may be painful and hurtful to those involved, but over time, when the wounds heal, it may be that the divided church can be more effective in its ministry as separate fellowships.

We are called as God's people to work for unity. Unity delights God (Psalm 133) and is what we should seek within our fellowships and between our fellowships. Divisions should be avoided at all costs, unless the gospel itself is at risk.

2 John 7–13

Hold on to the truth

Those who in their teaching deny Jesus Christ as Saviour and God are deceitful. Their teaching is dangerous and must be vigorously resisted.

People outside of the church today tend to be apathetic about the truth of the gospel rather than intent on spreading false ideas. Nevertheless, we should not be lulled into a false sense of security, since the influences that were around in the first century seeking to disrupt the community of believers are still at work today. Their activities may be subtler and we may have greater difficulty discerning them, but we need to be aware that false teaching destroys God's people if it continues unchecked.

At the time when this letter was written there were travelling preachers who claimed to have the truth and to know the ways of God. Their teaching was based on a variety of ideas linked to Greek philosophy, which led them to deny the heart of the gospel. They denied that Jesus was the Christ, the Son of God come in human flesh, and that his death was an atoning sacrifice.

Having written about love and truth as the basis for Christian community, John points out why the false teaching is so dangerous. The nature of the false teaching is that it is not the truth, and if it is not the truth then it cannot lead to love, only lovelessness. The evidence for this is seen in John's first letter, where the false teachers left the community of believers having caused division and broken relationships.

There are many today who claim to have the truth and to be able to lead others forward in their lives. People can be persuasive and credible, but if they deny Christ then they are deceivers, not teachers of truth, and their ministries will lead to discord and friction rather than love and unity.

It appears harsh to describe these people as deceivers and antichrists and yet, genuine and sincere as they might be in their beliefs, that is what they are. The terms antichrist and deceiver refer to those who, on the impulse of the powers of this world, seek to undermine God's people and to destroy their faith and communities. The New Testament speaks of one final antichrist who will be a global power of evil at the end of time, but it also refers to many lesser antichrists, doing the devil's work, as the end times continue to the time of Jesus' second coming.

The believers are instructed in the firmest of comments to take care that they do not lose their faith and miss out on the reward that they look forward to in Christ. The idea of working for a reward sits uncomfortably with many who, knowing everything is from God's grace, feel that to be rewarded is unhelpfully close to believing that our actions or 'works' are of value for salvation.

Jesus spoke frequently about being rewarded if we remain faithful in our discipleship (for example Matthew 6:4, 6). The reward is not material or social. It is not to do with status or ambition; it is a spiritual reward. It is not clear precisely what form it will take, but the reward will be there for those who have persevered until the end. The warning to watch out and take care is not just linked to false teaching; it could equally relate to destructive influences of any kind. It is easy to be led off track and persuade yourself that something outside of God's will is acceptable. Many have fallen for the deception that sexual immorality must be right because it feels good and the couple are in love. That deception is common even amongst Christians. It is short term in its perspective, usually comes from lust not love, and reminds us that feelings are always a poor indicator of what is correct.

Verse 9 highlights the possibility of false progress. We can all progress spiritually in both faith and in character, but we cannot add to the gospel. The gospel is complete, and any addition to it comes from flawed human thinking. Those adding to the teaching of the gospel and seeming to be fast-track Christians were actually 'off the track' Christians. Their beliefs were false, and rather than moving others forward in their faith they showed themselves to be detrimental to progress in the gospel and had in fact abandoned the teachings of Christ.

As John has stated before, keeping to the truth that Jesus himself proclaimed and that the first Christians adhered to means knowing the Father and the Son. Those who teach differently cannot have a relationship with the Father through the Son, otherwise they would not say such things.

In verses 10 and 11 there is a firm instruction not to show hospitality to those who preach deceitfully. This appears to contradict other passages of scripture where hospitality is positively commended (Romans 12:13; Hebrews 13:2). However, the issue in the context of 2 John is that by extending hospitality to the deceitful preachers, believers would be endorsing and confirming their words. If a Christian offered accommodation to a travelling speaker then it implied that the traveller was in good standing and acceptable to the household. This is not an instruction to be mean to those who need shelter, but to be wise in not encouraging their ministry or giving unintended support to those who are undermining the work of the kingdom of God.

It is a helpful reminder to fellowships to be careful and thoughtful about whom they invite or accept to speak and teach. It is easy to be careless in such things and find that erroneous teaching creeps into the community of God's people.

John concludes this letter with a human touch, showing his affection for those to whom he writes. He longs to see them face to face. There is so much that cannot be shared in a letter. Being there, sharing in person is so much more significant than distant communication. In our world of text messaging, e-mails and voice mail, I hope we will not neglect the basic human need to talk things through face to face.

The final sentence of this letter is a greeting from the church of which John is currently a member to the sister church to which he writes.

Questions

1. Look up the following references about being rewarded: Matthew 5:12, 6:4, 16:27; 2 Timothy 4:7–8. Do you think all believers will receive the same reward or will some that have shown themselves particularly worthy receive a greater reward?
2. What are the most damaging influences in the church that may halt believers in their spiritual progress?

Would we recognize a messenger of the antichrist if he came to our church?

3. Modern technology, with its scope for global communication and instant messages, appears to be a great asset to the gospel. Why might that not be true and why might John's desire to talk face to face with his readers still be relevant today?

4. Does verse 10 mean that we should never invite Jehovah's Witnesses into our homes?

False teachers

False teachers are those who claim to be proclaiming the truth but are not, those who claim to be Christians or to know God but who don't. This is a more relevant issue today than ever, in these days of global communication and postmodern culture. There are many people promoting causes, values and belief systems of a whole variety of types. In the multitude of voices it is difficult to discern who are the false guides and who are the true teachers.

Some alternative medicine, counselling methods and meditation techniques and philosophies, as well as other religions and variations on Christian faith, are examples of the options that might appear constructive and helpful but are later discovered to be false teaching. Not that all alternative medicine or counselling methods are false teaching. There are Christian cults such as Mormonism, Jehovah's Witnesses and Christian Scientists who have a lot of ethical values that are based on Christian teaching and many beliefs and ideas that Christians would agree with. However, in some way or other they have distorted the truth that Jesus proclaimed, adding to it or embellishing it in some way so that it is no longer the gospel truth that is liberating and transforming.

Much of this teaching falls into the category of human error (2 Peter 2:3), although there are some cults that are almost certainly demonic in their inspiration (1 Timothy 4:1–2). One example is 'The Children of God' led by David Berg. This cult had an appearance of orthodoxy and spirituality, but in fact promoted sexual immorality and the leader used the guise of faith to take the wealth of the followers in order to lead a lavish lifestyle.

There is a recognition throughout the New Testament that there are false teachers (1 Timothy 4:1–3). Their teaching is valueless; it does not build up the fellowship or the individual (Colossians 2:20–23), and it can be destructive (2 Peter 2:1) and lead people astray (Acts 20:30).

As the letters of John suggest, false teaching can be discerned by its content, whether it acknowledges Jesus as the Son of God who came as both fully human and fully divine (1 John 4:2–3). False teaching can also be discerned by the teacher's lifestyle and the effect of the teaching on others. False teachers will be recognized by their fruits (Matthew 15:15–20) and their character, and the fruit of their ministry will indicate the source of their message. The fruit of the ministry of the false teachers that John wrote about was division, disharmony and broken relationships. That was clear evidence that theirs was not a message of truth. Other false teachers destroyed the faith of believers or simply got tied up in discussions and arguments that prevented God's work from being done (2 Timothy 2:16–18).

False teaching is cruel because it denies people the opportunity to know the full truth and transforming power of the gospel. Many who have thought they have stumbled on some 'new truth' and presented it as such have caused enormous hurt and pain. For example, those who have asserted that suffering is caused by lack of faith or that there is no room for mourning or sadness in the community of God's people have added to the hurt of people who are already in pain.

3 John 1–13

Be imitators of good

This third letter of John helps us to reflect on how we support those called to Christian ministry. It gives us an example of poor leadership and two examples, Gaius and Demetrius, of godly living.

This third letter from John is full of affection and spiritual concern. John again (see 2 John 1) refers to himself by the term elder, meaning a friend senior in years but gracious and close in relationship. We don't precisely know who Gaius was. It was a common name at the time. Tradition has thought him to be one of the leaders of the church at Pergamum.

It is intriguing to discover that what I thought was a very English habit of asking after someone's health and wishing them well is in fact an ancient custom. The writer shows that he wants the best for his friend in all ways, physically and spiritually. It is good to pray for physical health as long as we are also praying for spiritual health. We should not conclude from this that it is always right to pray for and expect good health, as that may not always be God's plan. Timothy (1 Timothy 5:23) had a health problem that God did not heal, and Paul knew what it was to suffer (2 Corinthians 12:7), as God allowed some troublesome aspect of his life to remain in order to keep him humble.

Some have sought to build on verse 2 the argument that Christians should enjoy healthy living and prosperity as the right of God's people. They also point to the message of Deuteronomy, for example in Deuteronomy 5:33, that God intended his people to take over the land and enjoy prosperity and peace. Such teaching ignores the references to suffering with Christ and sharing the scorn and derision of being set apart for God (Philippians 1:29; Hebrews 13:13).

Gaius was an example and an encouragement, a man who was faithful to the truth and continuing in the truth. For John, who heard discouraging news of division and failure, it was good to be reminded of the dependable and committed disciple of Christ who maintained the faith steadfastly.

This letter gives us an interesting insight into leadership in the early church. There is no one clear pattern of church leadership in the New Testament; a variety of models of church leadership existed. This letter indicates how the early church in one area operated. There were local leaders like Gaius and Diotrephes (verse 9). There were travelling preachers and teachers (verse 5), and there were also the Apostles such as John.

Gaius has shown support and welcome to the travelling teachers. John is grateful for that and affirms the life and ministry of Gaius. Together they are built up in their faith and hope in Christ. Prayer is central to their relationship and community. They pray for each other and see God answer their prayers as they are built up to be the people of love and truth to which they are called. What we have is a picture of a loving community where there is mutual support and encouragement.

Travelling preachers were a common feature of the early church. Inns were not appropriate places for a Christian to stay, as they were places of poor reputation where coarse behaviour and immorality were common. Itinerant Christian teachers needed to find accommodation with local Christians if they were to be able to carry out their ministry. Gaius had shown himself to be a considerate and supportive host whose hospitality to the travelling Christians had been heard of by John himself. The only material support that these Christian workers would have had was from the fellowship of other believers. They did not accept or did not receive support from non-Christians.

The work of Christian ministry today continues under the same principle as it did in the first century, although the actual practice has changed. Those in Christian ministry need to be supported and cared for if they are to be able to carry out their work. It is the fellowship of other believers who offer either hospitality or financial support. God's work cannot go forward without this sharing of resources.

Gaius is affirmed and commended for his example and behaviour, but Diotrephes (verse 9) is condemned for his. Diotrephes appears to be the kind of character who has to be first and whose arrogance and pride leads to unfortunate and misguided judgments. Diotrephes had far too much concern for himself and seemed unable to share leadership with others. He may well have been the leader of the community to which Gaius belonged, which is why John wrote to Gaius, knowing that Diotrephes would try to prevent the letter being widely heard.

Diotrephes is roundly criticized for his inability to be accountable to others or to submit to others. He appears to be a thoroughly unpleasant character who is not only self-important but who also gossips maliciously and is mean spirited and suspicious of Christian visitors. He appears to be a heavy-handed leader with an autocratic approach who puts out of the fellowship anyone who shows basic hospitality and care to those of whom he does not approve. It would seem he operates a closed fellowship where only those who are known and presumably submit to him are accepted.

Leadership in the church is as crucial an issue today as it was in the time when 3 John was written. Christian leaders should be accountable to God and submitted to his Lordship, and they should care for the spiritual well-being of those for whom they have responsibility. Good leadership follows the pattern of Christ, of being a servant, of being prepared to lay down their lives for the sake of their followers. Good leadership is concerned not to take power and to become controlling, but to draw out the strength and potential of others. Good leadership is about seeing the whole community built up, not just the reputation of the leader. Diotrephes failed at every point. The example of John in his letters is a positive model of leadership as he guides and directs, showing love and humility.

Gaius and those who read the letter with him were encouraged not to be influenced by Diotrephes, but to follow only the patterns of good leadership with which they had become familiar. John's condemnation of Diotrephes reaches a climax as he implies that Diotrephes does not know God, otherwise he would behave more acceptably.

This is a familiar theme for John in his epistles: those who do good prove they are God's children, and those who do evil prove that they are not (1 John 3:7–10). The test of faith is how we live and our character. We are saved by faith alone, but the faith that saves brings with it a desire to live a godly life and reflect Christ in our lifestyle and character.

Having spoken negatively about Diotrephes, John returns to positive news and speaks about Demetrius. We do not know too much about Demetrius. We cannot be sure what his role or status was in the church, but what we do know is that he was widely recognized as being a person full of the truth of God. In other words, he was someone in whom God's presence was seen and from whom the truth of God flowed. We can all recall people we have met who have been like that, those who are a blessing to be with and who build us up in our faith by their presence amongst us. Our prayer for ourselves should be that we might be thought of like Demetrius and be able to minister to others as he did.

The final verses of this letter remind us again of how much easier it is to talk face to face. How much more rewarding such conversations and discussions can be. We see the homely side of John as he reveals how much he wants to see Gaius personally so he can be encouraged and share other news.

The final blessing consists of familiar words that the God of peace might be with him. He wishes his friend the wholeness and completeness that is only found in God through Christ. This is not a peace that takes away all the storms of life, but a peace within the pressures and a perspective that recognizes that all we pass through has a purpose for his glory.

John shares greetings from friends he is with, and wishes his greetings to go to all the friends with Gaius, much as we might do when writing to someone today.

Questions

1. Do you think the leadership behaviour of Diotrephes is a common occurrence in Christian communities today? How can a church congregation ensure it does not have a leader like Diotrephes?
2. How does your fellowship support those called to Christian ministry? Are there ways in which your fellowship could be more effective in its support?
3. Are there Christian friends who you regularly pray for and who pray for you? Should you develop more relationships of trust and encouragement such as John and Gaius had?

The prosperity gospel

Those who base their teaching on the doctrines that have come to be known as 'the prosperity gospel' teach that if you follow Christ as they suggest you will have wealth, health and success. The thought behind their teaching is that many people are put off becoming Christians because they believe that they will have to pay too high a price. The good news they spread is that God wants them to be prosperous, but they have got to get right with him first.

They quote many Bible references such as Matthew 6:33, 'But seek first his kingdom and his righteousness, and all these things will be given to you as well', to support their claims. In essence they believe that those who give generously to God's work will be blessed with material prosperity and physical well-being. Prosperity and good health are taken to be signs that God approves and are often held up as proof of God's generous provision for those who love Him!

The contrary is unfortunately also taken to be true. Any form of poverty or ill health is a sign that a believer is not being blessed by God. The remedy to the situation usually involves the believer doing one or more of the following:

▶ Increasing their levels of faith

▶ Making sure that they have paid at least ten per cent of their income to the church

▶ Ensuring there is no area of sin in their lives

▶ Avoiding any kind of negative or discouraging thought; whatever they want they have to 'name it and claim it'

▶ Not becoming disheartened when somebody else gets the blessing they have been seeking from God

Churches who focus on prosperity issues are preoccupied with being winners in every aspect of life, particularly in the area of finances.

It is a subtle heresy because it appears biblical in that it takes a selection of isolated verses, such as 3 John 2, and interprets them in a materialistic manner. The Old Testament promises of occupying the land and being blessed with long life and prosperity are also emphasized.

What the prosperity teachers fail to acknowledge is all the biblical references that relate to suffering with Christ and not being lovers of money or tempted by the attraction of worldly possessions. The balanced biblical view is that wealth is a good gift from God and, particularly under the old covenant, is a blessing to the faithful and believing. However, even under the old covenant the obedient and godly suffered and faced ordeals of many kinds.

We only need to look at the experience of Job to understand that.

The new covenant through Christ focuses much more on spiritual riches and wealth in heaven, and recognizes that as God's people we may well go through tough times and suffering, we may experience poverty, illness and pain. It is by God's grace that we are sustained through these times and experience his strength. We also understand that often it is the way of suffering that teaches us most about our need of God, when we learn to rely most heavily on his spiritual resources and realize the inadequacy of material resources. Often Jesus delivers us not *from* suffering, but *in* it and *through* it, just as happened to him.

For further reading

There are a number of books which cover the issues of the letters of John if you wish to study further. These are a few that you might find helpful.

Colin G. Kruse, *The Letters of John* (The Pillar New Testament Commentary), 2000. A commentary designed for the serious student of the biblical text and those general readers who wish to have a deep understanding illuminated by contemporary scholarship and pastoral sensitivity.

Michael Eaton, *1.2.3. John* (Christian Focus), 1994. A commentary that gives a good insight into the essential focus of these letters. It is practical Bible exposition and there is an emphasis on relevantly applying the Bible to real situations.

David Jackman, *The Letters of John* (IVP Bible Speaks Today Series), 1988. A study in the letters of John aimed at the preacher and Bible teacher. There is depth and clarity for the committed reader in this volume.

Simon Jones, *Discovering the New Testament* (IVP Crossway Bible Guide), 2001. A survey of the New Testament, putting the letters of John in the wider context. This book is useful as an individual study guide or for groups.